THE

# OREGON
## SKYLINE TRAIL

# THE
# OREGON
# SKYLINE TRAIL

*A HISTORY*

## GLENN VOELZ

THE
History
PRESS

Published by The History Press
Charleston, SC
www.historypress.com

Copyright © 2024 by Glenn Voelz
All rights reserved

First published 2024

Manufactured in the United States

ISBN 9781467157056

Library of Congress Control Number: 2024930886

# CONTENTS

# ACKNOWLEDGEMENTS

Oregon's Skyline Trail has a long and sometimes complicated history. Piecing the story together required the help of many collaborators. Numerous talented historians have done invaluable work on various aspects of the story. They include Paul Sutter, Gerald Williams, Stuart Barker, Martin Winch, Terence Young, Silas Chamberlin, Robert Cox, David Lewis, William Tweed, Lawrence and Mary Rakestraw and Harold Steen.

Several individuals went above and beyond to offer their help on the project. Barney Scout Mann shared his vast knowledge of trail history, including his fascinating research on early "thru-hikers." Jason McInteer, the Heritage Program manager for the Willamette National Forest, helped track down Fredrick Cleator's 1920 Skyline Trail diary and trip report. Mekia Ogborn and Steve Lent of the Bowman Museum and Vanessa Ivey of the Deschutes County Historical Museum were always willing to indulge my random inquiries and picture requests.

Jim O'Connor of the U.S. Geological Survey was incredibly generous in sharing his research and images from Frederick Cleator's 1920 survey. Lauren Goss, Julia Simic and Randy Sullivan from the University of Oregon's Special Collections and University Archives provided invaluable assistance with documents and photographs from the Frederick Cleator and John Breckenridge Waldo papers. Anna Dvorak and Rachel Lilley from the Special Collections and Archives Research Center at Oregon State University helped me navigate and access the Gerald W. Williams papers.

I'm grateful to Scott Daniels and Robert Warren at the Oregon Historical Society, who have always provided excellent support and advice. Mathew Brock at the Mazama Library has been another indispensable resource on this and other projects. I would especially like to thank Les Joslin for numerous discussions over coffee and for sharing his endless knowledge about U.S. Forest Service history.

Many organizations and individuals generously provided images used in the book. These include the Oregon Historical Society, the U.S. Forest Service, the Forest History Society, the Washington State Parks and Recreation Commission, the Willamette Falls & Landings Heritage Area Coalition, the Appalachian Trail Conservancy, the Mazama Library, the University of Oregon, Oregon State University, the Pacific Crest Trail Association, CCC Legacy, the Bancroft Library at UC Berkeley, the University of Wisconsin–Madison, the U.S. Library of Congress, the U.S. Geological Survey, the National Park Service, the Deschutes County Historical Society, the Bowman Museum, James O'Conner, Daniel Karnes, June Mulford and Deems Burton.

Several readers, including Les Joslin, Barney Scout Mann and Susan Conrad, reviewed the manuscript and provided suggestions for improvement. While the project could not have happened without the help of many, any mistakes and errors are my own.

*Leave the road, take the trail.*

*—Pythagoras*

# INTRODUCTION

In July 1920, U.S. Forest Service forester Frederick Cleator set out from Crater Lake on a four-month assignment to scout and map a recreational route along Oregon's Cascade Crest. His team included nine horses, a government packer, a road engineer, two grazing experts and a cook. In addition to their camping kit, the team carried surveying equipment, photography gear and even carrier pigeons for communication. Cleator's task was to survey the path for a scenic highway, known as the Skyline Road, connecting Mount Hood to Crater Lake.

The idea for the highway emerged during a period of ambitious roadbuilding projects around the state amid enthusiasm for a new age of automobile-based tourism. Boosters promised that the Skyline Road would open the High Cascades for recreation and become one of the "greatest scenic drives" in the country.[1] Although the scenic highway was never built, the route Cleator blazed that summer eventually became the centerpiece of America's greatest long-distance hiking trail.

When Cleator set out to survey and map the Skyline route, there was only a handful of developed hiking trails in the United States, mostly on the East Coast. The Appalachian Trail had not even been formally proposed when Cleator began his work. At the time, the Forest Service was just beginning to embrace the idea of promoting recreation on National Forest System lands. Cleator was one of the agency's first recreational planners and personally oversaw the development of much of the early recreational infrastructure in Oregon's national forests.

Although Cleator was the first to formally scout and map the Skyline route, the trail had a long history, spanning thousands of years. It began as an intermittent footpath used by Oregon's Indigenous tribes to access seasonal encampments and facilitate trade among tribal bands separated by the High Cascades. By the mid-nineteenth century, Euro-American trappers and explorers used the same trails to cross the mountains into the Willamette Valley.

Early Oregon pioneers like Felix Scott, John Craig, William Odell and John Minto followed those same paths as they scouted the first wagon routes over the Cascade Crest. By the 1880s, stockmen frequented the unnamed trails to move their sheep and cattle to high alpine meadows for summer grazing. Around the same time, Oregonians began venturing into the mountains for recreation and leisure.

One of the first people to explore the length of the Oregon Cascades was Judge John Breckenridge Waldo. For twenty-seven summers starting in the late 1870s, Waldo covered most of what would become the Skyline Trail route. Over those years, Waldo became a passionate advocate for protecting the Cascades. He spent decades battling the powerful grazing and timber interests that were trying to exploit the forests for commercial gain. Waldo was a leading force in the creation of the Cascade Range Forest Reserve, a contiguous, protected wilderness stretching between Mount Hood and Crater Lake.

Before the Skyline Trail had a name, other prominent Oregonians— men like Henry Yelkus, Dee Wright, Cy Bingham and Lige Coalman— traveled its path and left their mark on the route. By the start of World War I, several sections of the trail had been informally established, though not thoroughly mapped. In 1919, the Forest Service proposed developing the route as a recreational attraction for auto tourism. The idea initially had strong support among the state's business interests, newspapers and fledgling tourism industry. However, the challenges of rugged landscape, persistent snowpack and high development costs ultimately rendered the highway project infeasible.

As the Forest Service pursued other recreational projects, trail development stalled. During the 1920s, the route remained difficult to access for all but the hardiest adventurers. Nevertheless, it became a popular backcountry escape for hunters, anglers and outing clubs like the Mazamas and the Obsidians. The remote mountain footpath even inspired books, poems, photo exhibits and travelogues. Bend's famous ski club, the Skyliners, would take its name from the trail.

After 1921, when the trail was mapped and posted, a few eccentric adventurers attempted to cover the route in uninterrupted journeys, but these early thru-hikers were few and far between. By the start of the Great Depression, most of the route remained unimproved, and the Forest Service abandoned the idea of building a scenic highway. However, the nation's deep economic crisis had a silver lining for the Skyline Trail.

New Deal–era work programs intended to help stabilize the economy brought thousands of young men into the Cascades as part of the Civilian Conservation Corps (CCC). Work crews known as "Roosevelt's Tree Army" went into Oregon's national forests and helped build much of the state's early recreational infrastructure, including campgrounds, trails and resorts. At the same time, the Forest Service began designating tracts along the Skyline route as primitive areas that would preserve much of the adjacent wilderness in perpetuity.

As the CCC crews worked in the forests, businessman Clinton Clarke began an effort to create a long-distance hiking trail from Canada to Mexico. Oregon's Skyline Trail would form the linchpin of that project, connecting a series of existing trails through Washington and California. Clarke enlisted the support of YMCA groups who reconnoitered the entire route during the mid-1930s. But following a surge of activity during the New Deal era, the Skyline Trail was largely forgotten during World War II as recreation slowed and the Forest Service focused on supporting the war effort.

The postwar years brought a renewed interest in outdoor recreation, camping and hiking. As Oregonians went to the forests in search of adventure and relaxation, the government attempted to balance the needs of many users while also satisfying changing expectations for environmental protection. That led to the establishment of new wilderness areas along the Skyline Trail route and, eventually, its designation as a National Scenic Trail within the Pacific Crest Trail System in 1968.

# I

# A NATURAL AND CULTURAL HISTORY
# OF THE OREGON CASCADES

A journey along Oregon's Skyline Trail is a tour through the region's complex geologic landscape formed over millions of years. The trail's path runs adjacent to the Cascade Crest, extending some three hundred miles from the Columbia River to Crater Lake. The Oregon section of the Cascade Range averages around five thousand feet of elevation, punctuated with numerous peaks rising above nine thousand feet. The range is nearly ninety miles wide in some spots and encompasses roughly 17 percent of the state's landmass. It contains many of Oregon's most dramatic natural landmarks, including Mount Hood, Mount Jefferson, the Three Sisters and Crater Lake.

The Cascades formed through the movements of an offshore subduction zone where the Juan de Fuca tectonic plate descends beneath the North American plate. The movement of those plates generates earthquakes around the subduction zone and magmatism (the motion of magma) parallel to the convergent boundaries. The line of magmatism from the Cascadia Subduction Zone extends from British Columbia to northern California. Volcanos are the surface expression of this phenomenon.

From a geologic perspective, the Cascade Range has two distinct parts: the Western Cascades and the High Cascades. The Western Cascades experienced an earlier period of volcanic activity.[2] Much of the visible evidence from that period has been erased by years of erosion and covered with dense vegetation. The prominent topographic features of the Western Cascades are approximately thirty million years old.

In contrast, the High Cascades experienced a much later period of volcanic activity as the crest gradually shifted eastward. The younger portion of the Cascades is approximately three million years old. But some spots reveal evidence of more recent volcanic activity, including features only a few thousand years old. Today, the volcanos of the Western Cascades are extinct, while many in the High Cascades remain active.

One of the High Cascade's most famous features, Crater Lake, was formed after the eruption and collapse of Mount Mazama some 7,700 years ago. Over centuries, rain and snowfall filled the caldera to its depth of 1,950 feet, making it the deepest lake in the United States. Crater Lake holds the most water of any lake in Oregon.[3]

Two types of volcanos dominate Oregon's Cascade Range. The first type is the steep-sided composite volcano, known as a stratovolcano. These tall, symmetrical volcanos formed over a long period, built on layers of lava flows, volcanic ash and cinders. Many of Oregon's notable peaks were created as composite volcanos. These include Mount Hood, Mount Jefferson, the Three Sisters, Broken Top and the collapsed Mount Mazama, now filled by Crater Lake.

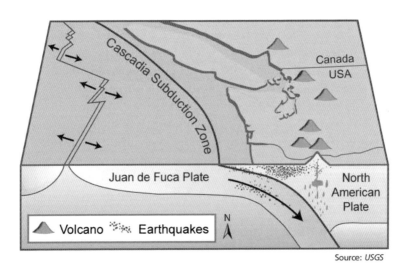

Source: *USGS*

The Juan de Fuca Plate subducting beneath the edge of North America created Oregon's Cascades Range and a string of dramatic volcanos stretching from northern California to southern British Columbia. *U.S. Geological Survey.*

The volcanic history of the Cascades written across the landscape. An aerial view of the Three Sisters region. *Photograph by Lyn Topinka. U.S. Geological Survey.*

A second type of volcano found along the range is the shield volcano. These tend to have a lower profile with gentle slopes that form a convex shape as they flatten near the summit. Their distinct structure is caused by repeated eruptions of fluid lava occurring intermittently over a long period. This allows for the gradual accumulation of volume that can reach enormous dimensions. Prominent examples of shield volcanos include Belknap Crater, Mount Bachelor, Mount Thielsen and Mount McLoughlin.[4]

Much of the Cascade Range has been shaped by ancient glacial activity. During the last Ice Age, from about 1.8 million to about 10,000 years ago, nearly all of the state's mountainous areas over six thousand feet of elevation were covered by glaciers.[5] As recently as 20,000 years ago, a contiguous sheet of ice covered much of the area between Mount Jefferson and Mount McLoughlin.[6] Today, most Cascade glaciers have disappeared, except for a few at the highest elevations on Mount Hood, Mount Jefferson and in the Three Sisters.

Evidence of ancient glacial dynamics is particularly notable in the foothills of the Western Cascades where steep, narrow valleys were carved by moving ice. Other signs of glacial movement can be seen throughout the High Cascades in the bowl-shaped depressions called cirques and the piles of loose sediment and rock debris known as moraines. Numerous lakes scattered around the range were formed as terminal moraines prevented meltwater from escaping those depressions. Some notable examples of this phenomenon are Crescent, Odell, Cultus and Suttle Lakes.

## THE CASCADE RANGE ECOREGION

The Cascades Range divides Oregon into two distinct climate zones. The western part of the state generally experiences milder temperatures and higher amounts of rainfall, with annual precipitation averaging 70 to over 150 inches. On the eastern side, the climate is more extreme: warmer in the summer and colder in the winter. Rainfall on the eastern side of the range averages around 12 inches annually, most of which comes during wintertime.[7] The average streamflow off the Western Cascades is approximately ten times that of the eastern slopes.[8]

The foothills of the Western Cascades are characterized by steep, narrow valleys, often covered with deep snowpack in the winter. Mature soil along the western slopes supports dense stands of hemlock, red cedar and Douglas fir.[9] As one moves higher into the mountains, the topography transitions to an undulating volcanic plateau dotted with buttes, cinder cones and glacial lakes. The forests of this region are dominated by mountain hemlock and silver fir, rising to an elevation of around 6,500 feet.

Above the high plateau is the subalpine and alpine ecoregion defined by glaciated volcanic peaks rising as high as eleven thousand feet. The highest elevation of the alpine zone experiences a harsh winter climate. In that zone, the sparse vegetation is adapted to deep snow, cold temperatures and a short growing season. Vegetation is limited to hardy shrubs, mountain hemlock and subalpine fir. Scattered patches of endangered whitebark pines survive at elevations up to around seven thousand feet.[10] In recent years, the whitebark pine has been devastated by fungal disease, bark beetle infestation and climate change. It's now classified as a threatened species.

Areas east of the Cascade Crest are in a rain shadow and receive much less precipitation than the western slopes. The eastern slopes experience more significant temperature variation and are prone to wildfires. Hemlock, fir and whitebark pine are common at higher elevations, while ponderosa and lodgepole pine are found at lower elevations. The eastern slope of the Cascades had less glacial activity and erosion than the western side. Thus, the eastern valleys are less steep and have fewer streams. The landscape along the foothills is dotted with volcanic buttes, cinder cones and lava flows.

Water from the Cascades flows into several different drainage basins. The headwaters of the streams roughly define the boundary between the Western and the High Cascades. Runoff from the northern portion of the western range flows into the Willamette Basin and eventually into the Columbia River, which is the only waterway bisecting the Cascades from east to west.

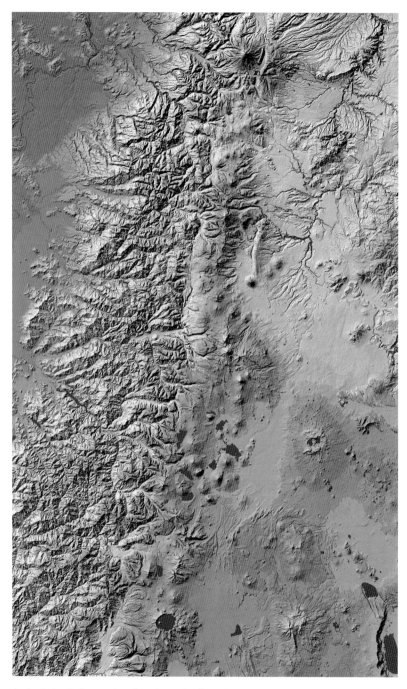

A shaded relief map showing the path of the Skyline Trail along the Oregon Cascades from Mount Hood to Crater Lake. *U.S. Geological Survey.*

The major tributaries in the northwestern portion of the range include the Middle Fork of the Willamette, the McKenzie, the Santiam, the Molalla and the Clackamas Rivers. Runoff from the southwestern portions of the range flows into the southern coastal basin, forming the Rogue and the South and North Umpqua Rivers. These rivers flow through the coastal range directly to the Pacific Ocean.

Water from the eastern side of the range flows into two major basins. The northern section flows into the Deschutes Basin watershed. The upper Deschutes River originates in the Cascades at Little Lava Lake. The lake is fed by inflow from groundwater reservoirs charged by the melting snowpack from Mount Bachelor and the Three Sisters area. The river flows south into Crane Prairie Reservoir, then into Wickiup Reservoir before turning north and eventually joining the Columbia River.

The southern portion of the eastern range drains into the Klamath River basin, which eventually flows south before turning west to the Pacific Ocean.[11] However, some runoff from the southwestern range flows into the closed basin of southern Oregon, where it is lost to evaporation or absorbed as groundwater.

## INDIGENOUS ORIGINS OF THE SKYLINE TRAIL

Since the beginning of human occupation in Oregon, the Cascade Range has defined the cultures of those living in its shadows. Archaeologic evidence suggests that humans have lived on the flanks of the mountains at least since the later part of the Pleistocene, around 11,700 years ago. At the end of the Ice Age, approximately 10,000 years ago, the glaciers began retreating. Around this time, the higher-elevation regions of the Cascades became accessible for travel and seasonal rounds.

The Columbia River Gorge is the only natural passage through the mountains, and routes over the crest were impassable for much of the year. Thus, the Cascades were a formidable natural barrier demarcating different cultural, linguistic and lifestyle patterns. The resource-rich western side supported larger communities that subsisted through hunting, gathering and fishing. The eastern side of the mountains was a dryer, more resource-poor ecosystem better suited to smaller communities able to move seasonally to access resources.

The area around The Dalles and Celilo Falls on the Columbia River was the epicenter of a regional trade network that existed for thousands of

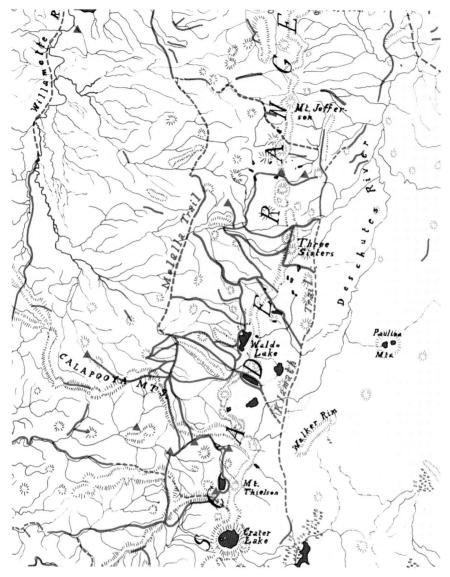

The Native American trail systems of the Oregon Cascades. Original map by Daniel Karnes, based on historic maps and records of the *Government Land Office. Used with permission.*

years before Euro-American colonization.[12] The site was one of the most productive fishing areas in the Pacific Northwest, generating an enormous supply of dried salmon that was the foundation for a complex network of commercial interactions running the length of the Cascade Range. When the Lewis and Clark expedition passed by the falls in the spring of 1806,

Clark called it the "Great Mart of all this Country," given the vast amount of trade among the tribes.[13]

In addition to salmon, tribes from across the Pacific Northwest and Columbia Plateau came to the site to exchange furs, baskets, clothing, beads and obsidian. A trail network running along the length of the Cascades facilitated these exchanges. The wide distribution of obsidian sourced from Central Oregon hints at the vast expanse of these trans-Cascadian trade networks, extending as far north as British Columbia and south into California.[14] The main trails running parallel to the Cascades crossed the mountains at various points. These higher-elevation trails were used for seasonal rounds, providing access to subalpine forests and meadows for hunting and gathering during the summer months.

At the onset of Euro-American contact, the size of Oregon's Indigenous population was likely somewhere between 50,000 and 100,000 people.[15] That population included significant linguistic, economic and cultural diversity adapted to Oregon's varied ecology. The Cascade Range was a de facto boundary separating Oregon's Indigenous groups.

On the western side of the mountains, the Molalla peoples ranged across the Cascade foothills from Mount Hood to Mount McLoughlin.[16] The Molalla homeland was linked by a network of trails from the Clackamas River extending as far south as the Umpqua and Rogue River basins. The trail system had numerous branches leading into and across the range.[17]

Due to the harsh winter conditions at higher elevations, the Molallas spent winters in the Cascade foothills. They traveled to the mountains during summer to hunt game and gather huckleberries. The Southern Molallas maintained close ties with the Klamath people, who resided on the elevated plateau on the southeastern side of the mountains. The two groups used a network of trails crossing the Cascades to facilitate trade and visitation.[18]

Like the Molalla, the Klamath ventured into the Cascades during summer to hunt and gather berries using a network of trails stretching between Mount McLoughlin and Crater Lake. As the Klamath expanded their trade relations with groups along the Columbia, they used a north–south trail system running along the eastern side of the Cascades, now known as the Klamath Trail. That route began east of Crater Lake and tracked to the north between the Cascade foothills and Deschutes River. The path had branches going west over the mountains at various points, connecting with Northern Molalla settlements on the other side. On the western side of the Cascades, the Molalla Trail was another north–south network extending along the eastern foothills of the Willamette Valley.

One of the more important branches of the Klamath Trail crossed the mountains near the present-day Santiam Pass and continued along the North Santiam River.[19] Indigenous groups likely used these routes to move enslaved people who were traded between the Klamath Basin and the Willamette Valley in the early nineteenth century.[20]

The complex network of Indigenous trails along and over the Cascades evolved over generations. The accounts of early Euro-American explorers and trappers are filled with notes about these Native footpaths.[21] Their maps depict Indigenous trails that eventually became the routes used by early settlers crossing the mountains into the Willamette Valley. Long sections of what became the Oregon Skyline Trail were based on these early routes, which had been used for thousands of years before the start of Euro-American settlement.[22]

## Early Euro-American Exploration into the Cascades

The Cascades posed a dominating geophysical boundary separating the region's Indigenous tribes. Rugged terrain and snow-covered passes meant that the higher elevations were accessible only a few months of the year. The mountains presented a similar challenge for early Euro-American explorers, who spent decades searching for passable routes over the range.

Peter Skene Ogden was one of the first Euro-Americans to explore the edges of the Cascades. Between 1824 and 1830, Ogden made half a dozen explorations across the American West while trapping and trading on behalf of the Hudson's Bay Company. In the fall of 1825, he led a party south from the Columbia River into Central Oregon, following the general route of the Klamath Trail. That path took Ogden's party through present-day Madras, past Suttle Lake and into the Newberry Caldera.

During the expedition, two other Hudson's Bay Company trappers, Finan McDonald and Thomas McKay, left Fort Vancouver and traveled along the western slope of the range with orders to rendezvous with Ogden on the eastern side. The men followed a path up the South Santiam River, likely crossing the crest somewhere around Santiam Pass, then continued into the Klamath Basin.[23] They later met with Ogden near the present-day site of Warm Springs.[24] McDonald and McKay's journey was among the earliest documented trans-Cascadian crossings by non-Indigenous explorers.

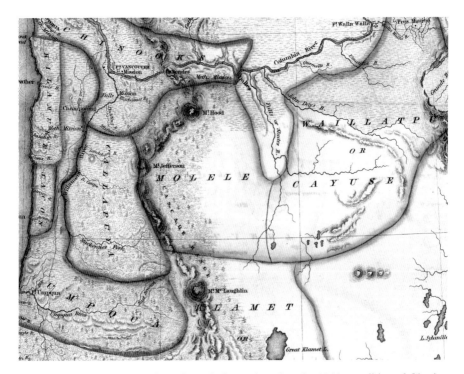

Map of Oregon Territory and the Cascade Range based on the 1844 expedition of Charles Wilkes. The map was one of the first to show the relative locations of Mount Hood, Jefferson and McLoughlin but revealed little information about the interior range. *U.S. Library of Congress.*

During later expeditions, Ogden was credited with being the first Euro-American to cross over the Siskiyou Pass between Oregon and California and to document Mount Shasta, the Klamath River and the Rogue and Umpqua River basins. Ogden's travels along the Cascade foothills brought him close enough to observe and document a rough outline of the range, providing vital geographic knowledge for subsequent expeditions.

Explorations of the late 1830s and early 1840s added important details to what was known about the Cascade topography. The U.S. Exploring Expedition of 1838–42, commanded by Lieutenant Charles Wilkes, used notes from Ogden's travels and other sources to create the 1841 Map of the Oregon Territory. It was the most accurate and detailed map of the region at the time.[25]

Wilkes's map depicted the locations of Mount Hood, Mount Jefferson and Mount McLoughlin, as well as several Indigenous trails crossing the Cascades. However, it offered few details about the range's interior,

Kit Carson and John Frémont (*pictured*) were guided by Billy Chinook of the Wasco tribe along the general route of the Klamath Trail while exploring Central Oregon in 1843. *Bowman Museum.*

which was still unexplored. In his notes, Wilkes warned that the mountain passes were "difficult and only to be attempted late in the spring and in the summer."[26]

In 1843, Captain John C. Frémont and Kit Carson added to the knowledge about the Cascades with their expedition on behalf of the U.S. Army Corps of Topographical Engineers. The purpose of the expedition was to survey and map the Oregon Trail from the Rocky Mountains. In December of that year, nineteen-year-old Billy Chinook of the Wasco tribe helped guide Frémont's party up the Deschutes River, following the old Klamath Trail. Early in the journey, while passing through the Tygh Valley, they noted a trail going west into the mountains and speculated that it might offer passage over the Cascades.[27]

When Frémont's party reached the present-day site of Warm Springs, they had a clear view of Mount Jefferson, Three Fingered Jack, Mount Washington and the Three Sisters, confirming their positions within the range. The party

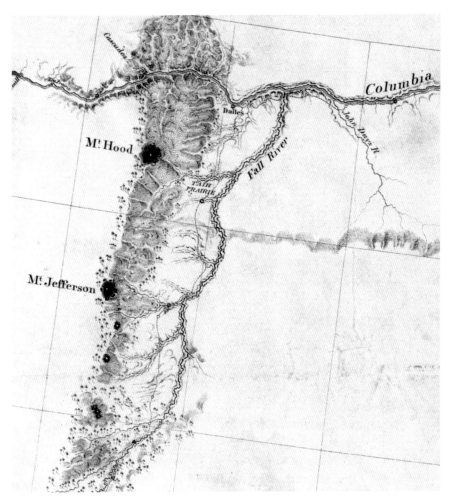

Map showing John Frémont's route along the eastern slope of the Cascades during the expedition of 1843–44. *U.S. Library of Congress.*

continued along the eastern foothills through Central Oregon as far south as Klamath Marsh before turning east toward Summer Lake.[28]

As Frémont's expedition explored the eastern slopes, early settlers in the Willamette Valley were already searching for viable wagon routes over the mountains from the west. In 1845, Thomas McKay, who had made an earlier trans-Cascade crossing, received a charter from the territorial legislature to establish a toll road leading up the South Santiam River and over the mountains.[29] Although McKay probably knew the terrain as well as any settler in Oregon Territory, he never blazed a permanent route through the Cascades.

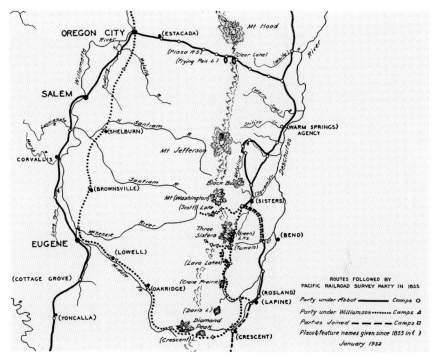

Routes of Lieutenants Henry Larcom Abbot and Robert Williamson during the 1855 Pacific Railroad Survey. Map by Robert Sawyer. *Oregon Historical Society.*

A decade later, Lieutenants Henry Larcom Abbot and Robert L. Williamson led one of the first expeditions pushing higher into the mountains as part of the Pacific Railroad Survey of 1855. When Abbot received his orders to scout potential railroad routes over the Cascades, he had only recently graduated from West Point and never ventured far from the East Coast.[30] For much of the journey, he followed a similar route as Frémont's party along the eastern slopes of the Cascades. He hoped to discover a viable path over the mountains south of Mount Jefferson but ultimately determined that the location wasn't suitable for a railroad.

In August, Abbot's main party split up. For the next several weeks, Lieutenants Williamson, George Crook and Philip Sheridan explored high into the Upper Deschutes basin. The party began near present-day La Pine, crossing the Deschutes River and then continuing to Crane Prairie. They explored upstream to Little Lava Lake, eventually reaching the source of the Deschutes River and camping there at the end of August. While there, they explored the high country around Sparks and the Green Lakes and may have passed over the crest of the Cascades.

In early September, Williamson's party descended from the Three Sisters down the Whychus Creek drainage, rejoining Abbot near the present-day site of Sisters.[31] Williamson continued his explorations into mid-September, following a route from Sisters to the south of Black Crater before continuing into the lava fields around what is now known as McKenzie Pass. They explored as far as Scott Lake before returning to join the rest of the party near Sisters.

In late September, Williamson departed the Deschutes and took his men southwest to Crescent Lake, south of Diamond Peak, then along the Middle Fork of the Willamette past the present-day town of Oakridge.[32] They followed the general path of the Free Emigrant Road, also known as the "Elliott Cutoff," after Elijah Elliott, who had disastrously promoted the route to an ill-fated wagon train in the summer of 1853.

Meanwhile, Abbot led his separate party down the Deschutes, looking for a route over the Cascades to the south of Mount Hood. He departed the river in the Tygh Valley, near the present-day site of Maupin. On the advice of a local settler, Abbot hired a Native American guide named An-ax-shat. The young man didn't speak English but was familiar with a route through

View of Mount Hood from Tygh Valley during the 1855 Pacific Railroad Survey. Lithograph based on an original watercolor by Robert Young, who accompanied the expedition. *Oregon Historical Society.*

the mountains he had traveled as a child.[33] An-ax-shat led Abbot's party of seventeen men over the mountains to the banks of the Clackamas River near the present-day town of Estacada. At the end of an arduous journey, Abbot wrote in his diary, "I have little doubt that we all owe our lives to the fidelity of this Indian."[34]

Although Native Americans and early fur trappers had walked those routes before, Abbot and Williamson were among the first to document and map them in detail. In their final report to Congress, Abbot and Williamson noted the difficulty of navigating through the mountains given the steep ravines, thick vegetation and deep snow during much of the year.[35] Another decade would pass before a reliable route was established over the mid-Cascades, enabling the construction of a permanent wagon road connecting Central Oregon to the Willamette Valley.

## The Search for Permanent Routes
## Over the Cascades

Oregon's settlement was well underway by the 1850s, but most of the territory's population was clustered around small communities in the Willamette Valley. The interior of the Cascades was still largely unexplored. Most new settlers crossed the mountains using the Barlow Road, south of Mount Hood. However, a few attempted to cross the Cascades along unproven routes. These efforts often ended in disaster, such as with the Meek's Cutoff (1845), the Applegate Trail (1846) and the Elliot Cutoff (1853). Without permanent roads, the Cascades remained a formidable obstacle for those wishing to reach the Willamette Valley from the east.

In 1851, John Preston began the initial land survey of the Oregon Territory. His team focused on sectioning areas along the Willamette Meridian, leaving the High Cascades unmapped. The challenging work of surveying the high country wouldn't begin until the early twentieth century. Even by the 1920s, some of the more rugged portions of the Cascades had yet to be formally surveyed.[36]

John Preston's maps of the 1850s note the general outline of the range and the location of notable peaks but little else. Nevertheless, those rudimentary maps would profoundly affect the creation of the state's political boundaries as the mountains became the de facto line demarcating Oregon's newly formed counties. By 1860, the Cascade Crest formed the eastern borders of Multnomah, Clackamas, Marion, Linn, Lane, Douglas and Jackson Counties. Everything to the east of that line became part of the newly created Wasco County.

When Oregon achieved statehood in 1859, there was a push by the federal government to improve the east–west wagon routes over the Cascades. Congress enacted a law granting land allotments from the public domain to subsidize the development of military wagon roads by private investors.[37] This encouraged entrepreneurs to scout potential routes for toll roads crossing the mountains. The search for those routes almost always began with known footpaths following the river valleys into the mountains.

Information about these routes had been passed down from early missionaries in the Willamette Valley who knew about the traditional Indigenous trails crossing the mid-Cascades. Fur trappers used many of these paths during the 1830s and 1840s.[38] One such man was the French Canadian trapper Joseph Gervais, who settled in French Prairie around 1830. Gervais was among the first non-Indigenous Oregonians to regularly cross over the mountains following a footpath up the Santiam Valley long used by the Molalla tribes.[39]

Early Oregon pioneer and trailblazer Andrew Wiley scouted one of the first permanent crossings over the mid-Cascades linking the Willamette Valley to Central Oregon.[40] Wiley settled near the Sweet Home Valley in 1853 and was an experienced woodsman familiar with the western foothills. He was on good terms with the Kalapuyan Indians, who sometimes passed by his homestead on their seasonal rounds into the Cascades. From them, he learned about their routes leading into the mountains.[41]

Beginning in 1858, Wiley spent several summers scouting the South Santiam River, searching for a viable wagon route over the crest around Mount Washington. In 1859, Wiley set out on a scouting trip following a trail rumored to have been the site of a historical conflict between the Molallas and the Paiute.[42] Wiley's party became disoriented along Hackleman Creek, near the present-day site of Lost Prairie Campground on U.S. Highway 20.

Wiley hiked up a ridgeline and climbed a tree to regain his bearings. From that vantage point, he supposedly became the first Euro-American to

Andrew Wiley settled in the Sweet Home Valley in the early 1850s and scouted the first wagon road over Santiam Pass. *Bowman Museum.*

spot the Santiam Pass from the western side of the mountains. Although Wiley is often credited with scouting the route, he was certainly not the first person to make the crossing. His path over the mid-Cascades followed a network of traditional trails used for centuries by Native Americans and later by early fur trappers.

Wiley continued refining the route over subsequent summers, and in 1864 a group of investors formed the Willamette Valley and Cascade Mountain Road Company to develop it into a wagon road.[43] The path was initially known as "Wiley's Trail," crossing over the crest a few miles south of present-day US Highway 20. By 1868, the Wiley Trail went from Linn County to the Deschutes River and became one of the main early routes over the Central Cascades.

Around the same time, Oregon Trail pioneer and road developer Captain Felix Scott hoped to establish another route over the Cascades along the McKenzie River into Central Oregon. In 1862, he led a party of fifty men to clear a path along an old Indian trail that passed through Belknap Springs and continued along Scott Creek. The route went south of the lava fields, snaking between North Sister and Black Crater along what is now Scott Trail.[44] That path followed a similar route blazed by Henry Spalding in 1859, crossing the crest between the McKenzie Pass and the Obsidian Cliffs.[45]

In the early 1870s, John Templeton Craig proposed a slightly different route over the McKenzie Pass. Craig had been part of the party scouting the Scott Trail in the summer of 1862. But Craig was convinced that a lower elevation route was available by traversing over several miles of rugged lava south of Belknap Crater. He founded the McKenzie, Salt Springs, and Deschutes Wagon Road Company and opened a toll road along the route in the fall of 1872.[46] The course Craig selected runs close to the present-day path of the McKenzie Highway.

The new routes over the McKenzie and Santiam Passes offered safer passage over the mountains for residents of the mid–Willamette Valley. However, the rapidly growing population of the southern valley also needed access to the grasslands and minerals of central and southeastern Oregon. William Macy and John Diamond were among the first to blaze a route over that part of the Cascades in 1852.

The men began in the Willamette Valley, following an old Klamath Indian trail over the crest near what is now called Diamond Peak, then continued into the Klamath Basin.[47] In the spring of 1864, investors from the Eugene-Springfield area filed articles of incorporation and sold stock to finance a wagon road close to that route through Emigrant Pass south of

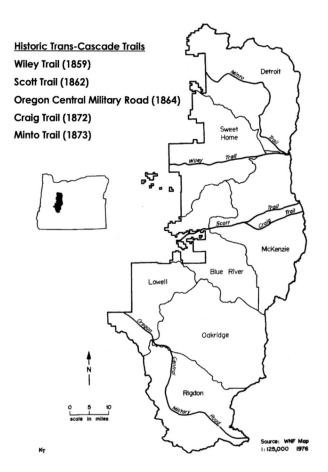

**Historic Trans-Cascade Trails**

**Wiley Trail (1859)**

**Scott Trail (1862)**

**Oregon Central Military Road (1864)**

**Craig Trail (1872)**

**Minto Trail (1873)**

Routes of the early trans-Cascade wagon roads. *Willamette National Forest.*

Diamond Peak.[48] Work began on the Central Oregon Military Wagon Road the following summer.[49]

A decade later, Bynon Pengra and William Odell scouted a new route crossing the Cascades to the south of the Free Emigrant Road around the present-day Willamette Pass. When that route was completed in the early 1870s, it still took seven to ten days of travel by wagon to reach the banks of the Upper Deschutes River from Eugene.[50]

By the 1870s, several wagon roads passed over the Cascades, but the search continued for better routes. One of those efforts was led by John Minto, who was born in England and came to Oregon in the migration of 1844. In the 1860s, he began a successful business raising pure-bred Merino sheep on a farm south of Salem. In the late 1860s, Minto's wife became ill, and on the advice of a doctor, the family began spending summers in the mountains. During those years, Minto became an expert on the flora, fauna and topography of the Cascades and knowledgeable about the history of the Indigenous tribes who had been crossing the mountains for centuries.[51]

In 1873, leaders in Marion County asked Minto to investigate the rumors about an old Indian trail over the mountains north of Three Fingered Jack.[52] The route went up the North Santiam River through present-day Detroit and Idanha before turning south around the base of Mount Jefferson. Minto claimed that he had heard about the trail directly from the French Canadian trapper Joseph Gervais, who used the passage during the 1830s and 1840s.[53]

In the late 1870s, there was brief consideration of developing Minto's route into a wagon road, but the pass was considerably higher than the one already scouted by Wiley years before. Today, that crossing point is known as Minto Pass, but it was never developed as anything more than a horse trail.

Yet another passage was scouted by Judge John Breckenridge Waldo, Oregon's first native-born state Supreme Court chief justice. Waldo grew up on a farm east of Salem and spent his youth exploring the Cascades between Mount Jefferson and the Three Sisters. He graduated from Willamette University in 1863 and studied law before joining the Oregon Supreme Court in 1880. He later represented Marion County in the state legislature.

Today, Waldo is sometimes referred to as "Oregon's John Muir" for his role as a chief proponent of creating the Cascade Range Forest Reserve. During the 1880s, Waldo spent several months each summer traveling the High Cascades between Mount Hood and Crater Lake. In 1880, he discovered a lower route over the crest several miles south of Minto Pass.[54] The spot was about three miles north of the route blazed by Andrew Wiley in 1859. Minto credited Waldo with identifying that passage around Hogg Rock, which would later become the path of U.S. Highway 20 when completed in 1929.

Both Minto and Waldo shared a deep love of the Cascades. The men spent years exploring and studying the range. But in later years, they were sharply divided over how to manage and protect it. The main divide was between those who saw the Cascades primarily as an economic resource and those who valued its natural beauty and hoped to preserve it for future generations. That debate became the context for the next chapter in the story of Oregon's Skyline Trail.

## 2

# BLAZING THE PATH

## *Judge Waldo and the Cascade Range Forest Reserve*

**B**y the early 1880s, several well-established routes over the Cascades offered starting points to begin explorations along the range's rugged spine. The northernmost of these passages was the Barlow Road, first scouted by Sam Barlow and Joel Palmer in the fall of 1845. The route began in The Dalles and then went south through the Tygh Valley before crossing the south shoulder of Mount Hood. Barlow's route partly followed an old Indian trail and cattle path cut by Daniel Lee.[55] After the pass, the route dropped to the Sandy River and eventually ran south of the Clackamas River to its terminus at Oregon City. Today's Mount Hood Highway follows much of Barlow's original route.

By the late 1880s, several routes over the mid-Cascades had been blazed around Santiam Pass by Andrew Wiley, John Minto, John Waldo and others. South of Mount Washington were routes over McKenzie Pass, established by Felix Scott and John Templeton Craig during the 1860s and 1870s. Another road over the mountains, known as the Central Oregon Military Wagon Road, linked Eugene to southeastern Oregon through the Klamath Basin.

Two trans-Cascades wagon roads through the southern reaches of the range were established by the U.S. Army in the 1860s to improve supply routes between Fort Klamath and outposts in the Rogue River Valley. The first of these, known as the "Rancheria Trail," was blazed in 1863. The trail started in Jacksonville and crossed over the northern slope of Mount McLoughlin. The trail proved too steep, however, and a different route was cut a few years later.[56]

The second passage was established in 1865 by Captain F.B. Sprague, U.S. Army. That route continued up the Rouge River to the present-day settlement of Union Creek.[57] From there, it went south of Castle Creek Canyon toward Crater Lake before crossing over the crest at 6,300 feet, paralleling Annie Creek Canyon to Fort Klamath. In the early twentieth century, when Crater Lake became a tourist destination, the wagon road became one of the main access routes into the national park, closely following the path of today's Oregon Highway 62.

To varying degrees, all these trans-Cascades routes followed Indigenous trails that had likely been used for thousands of years. Once established, these access points allowed more extended explorations along the Cascade Crest. But at that time, very little of the interior range had been scouted or mapped. One of the first Euro-Americans to embark on a thorough exploration along the High Cascades was Judge John Breckenridge Waldo.

## JUDGE WALDO BLAZES THE SKYLINE

During the 1880s, Judge Waldo spent his summers exploring the network of trails between Mount Hood and Crater Lake. His wanderings became the first step in establishing the general route of the Skyline Trail. More importantly, Waldo's explorations informed and inspired his lifelong advocacy for protecting the Cascade Range, spurring his campaign to make much of it federally protected forest reserves.

Waldo was born on a homestead in Marion County, east of Salem, in an area now known as the Waldo Hills. His parents had traveled to Oregon with the Applegate party in 1843 and settled in the Willamette Valley. Waldo had asthma as a child. To improve his health, Waldo spent his summers camping and fishing in the forests with his older brother William.

Waldo graduated from Willamette University in 1866 and was admitted to the Oregon state bar in 1870. As a young man, he began taking trips into the mountains in the early 1870s. His first crossing over the Cascades was in the summer of 1872 when he followed along the Central Oregon Wagon Road from Eugene, going as far as Davis Lake on the eastern side of the mountains.[58] During later forays into the High Cascades, Waldo often used the Wiley and Minto Trails to access the alpine forests around Mount Jefferson.

Over the years, Waldo became an experienced woodsman, often supplementing his dry food by fishing and hunting for deer, elk and bear.[59]

Judge John Breckenridge Waldo was likely the first Oregonian to travel the length of the future Skyline route during his explorations of the High Cascades in the late nineteenth century. *Oregon Historical Society.*

Waldo was a keen observer of nature and made detailed notes about the Cascades' flora, fauna and geology during his explorations. He occasionally noted the presence of grizzly bears and wolves, which, at the time, were still present in the Oregon Cascades. Waldo was well-read and broadly curious.

He carried volumes of Emerson, Thoreau, Darwin and Marcus Aurelius with him on his explorations into the mountains.[60]

In the summer of 1877, Waldo took an extended trip up the Santiam River to the present-day site of Marion Forks. From there, he spent a week exploring the slopes of Mount Jefferson.[61] A few years later, he scouted a different section of the future Skyline Trail route, covering the Three Sisters region, Elk Lake and the headwaters of the Deschutes River.

After his 1880 appointment to the Oregon Supreme Court, Waldo still managed to take summer trips into the high country, often for months at a time. He typically went with small groups of friends and moved through the mountains on horseback. During these expeditions, Waldo kept detailed diaries describing his daily routes and activities.[62] Those diaries reveal many of his favorite places, visited year after year, including Breitenbush Hot Springs, Odell Lake, Crane Prairie and Pengra Lake, later renamed Waldo Lake in his honor.

During the summer of 1881, Waldo returned to Mount Jefferson, camping at Pamelia Lake and exploring north into Jefferson Park. Much of the ground he covered that summer became the future route of the Skyline Trail. The following summer of 1882, Waldo turned south and followed the mountains from the Three Sisters south to Crater Lake. He visited the spot at a time when it was virtually unknown to most Oregonians and didn't appear on government maps. Waldo was taken aback by the experience, declaring it the most interesting spot he had visited in the mountains.[63]

When Waldo traveled in the mountains, he was keenly aware that he was following paths that had been used for centuries by Indigenous Oregonians. His attention to these details extended to his climbing escapades on some of Oregon's highest peaks. During the summer of 1883, Waldo was on his annual excursion with a friend named Adolph Dekum. The men had traveled from Eugene to Diamond Peak, then slowly worked north, making extended camps at Crescent and Davis Lakes before continuing into the Upper Deschutes Basin.

In early September, they camped at Lava Lake. They noted what they described as the Eastern, Northern and Western Sisters, likely referring to Bachelor Butte, Broken Top and South Sister, given their perspective. On September 9, Dekum wrote in his diary that they had summited the "easternmost" Sister, most likely Mount Bachelor, located a few miles north of their campsite at Lava Lake. Several days later, they scaled South Sister along the southeast ridgeline from the Green Lakes.

While climbing those peaks, Waldo and Dekum noted the presence of rock cairns piled several feet high. Dekum believed the cairns "seemed to have been piled up by human hands."[64] Dekum also found pieces of flint and wood slivers in a hole, indicating that Native Americans had likely visited both summits long before the Euro-American settlement. This frank admission ran counter to a prevailing prejudice at the time that Oregon's Indigenous people didn't venture to the top of the highest Cascade peaks.

The journals of John Frémont, one of the first Euro-Americans to explore Central Oregon, contained a prime example of this unexamined assumption. Frémont's diary of his 1843 expedition posited that "Indian superstition has peopled these lofty peaks with evil spirits, and they have never yet known the tread of human foot."[65] Apparently, Frémont didn't bother to ask his native guide, Billy Chinook, about the vast network of trails crossing over the mountains. In contrast, Waldo and Dekum were far more open-minded as they explored the High Cascades, always looking for signs of those who came before them.

Waldo continued his extended summertime journeys into the Cascades through the 1880s. During the summer of 1886, he spent several months covering the route from Mount Jefferson to Crater Lake and back. Along the way, Waldo summited several of the highest peaks, including Middle Sister, Mount Scott, Mount Thielsen, Mount Bailey and Diamond Peak.[66]

His travels during the next two summers were perhaps the most consequential for fixing the general route that would become the Skyline Trail. More importantly, those journeys preceded Waldo's election as a state representative. In that position, he would begin his campaign to create a protected forest reserve encompassing most of the Cascade Range.[67]

During the summer of 1887, Waldo planned a route from Jefferson Park to Mount Shasta, covering much of what became the Skyline Trail route. The party began on the Minto Trail at the end of July, with their first camps still covered in snow. Challenging conditions in the high country forced the party to reassess their goal of reaching Mount Shasta. Instead, they briefly diverted to the Metolius River before continuing their journey to Crater Lake.[68] After several months of travel, they crossed over the crest in early October near Summit Lake, south of Diamond Peak, just as the season's first snow arrived.

The following summer of 1888, Waldo planned to complete the southern portion of the journey to Mount Shasta, continuing the trip they had abandoned the year before. Their route along the crest would begin at Summit Lake, close to where they had left off the previous October. During

Rare photos of Judge Waldo's journeys into the Cascades. Waldo's pack train near the base of South Sister, 1889. *Special Collections & University Archives, University of Oregon.*

Waldo's campsite next to an unfinished log cabin after an early season snow, likely near Willamette Pass, 1889. *Special Collections & University Archives, University of Oregon.*

his years in the Cascades, Waldo had spent less time in the southern portion of the range, explaining his desire to see Mount Shasta.[69] The trip became a capstone of a decade spent exploring the High Cascades and clarified Waldo's thinking about preserving the range for future generations.

That summer, Waldo left his farm in early July, traveling through Coburg before crossing the McKenzie River and turning up the Middle Fork of the Willamette. He was joined by four other men, including Henry Minto, son of John Minto. As they traveled east into the mountains, Waldo revealed a bit of provincialism as they passed through various towns, observing that "Linn County is a very uninteresting County. Dreary and monotonous compared with Marion."[70]

They followed the Central Military Wagon Road over the mountains before making an extended camp at Davis Lake on the eastern side of the crest. The party remained in the area between Summit and Pengra (Waldo) Lakes for a few weeks before turning south in mid-August. They spent the next month blazing a trail from Summit Lake south to the California border. For the first part of the journey to Crater Lake, they took almost the exact route Frederick Cleator would use thirty years later during his 1920 Skyline survey.

One of Waldo's four companions during the 1888 trip was a young man named Felix Isherwood of Portland. During the journey, Isherwood carved the party's names on a series of trees at campsites along the way. While only a few of those "Waldo trees" still exist, Isherwood speculated some forty-five years later that the path they blazed that summer eventually became the route of the Skyline Trail.[71]

In late August, the party stopped to camp at Crater Lake and made a trip to Wizard Island, named just a few years before by William Gladstone Steel. In early September, they passed through the Sky Lakes Basin. By mid-month, the group made camp at Four Mile Lake and two days later climbed Mount McLoughlin, then known as Mount Pitt. Waldo wrote in his diary that, over those months, "the Cascade Mountains became our highway."[72]

In mid-September, they departed Lake of the Woods and continued to Old Baldy, now known as Mount Bailey, which they scaled several days later. By this point in the journey, they were able to catch glimpses of Mount Shasta to the south. By the twenty-third, they had reached Grass Valley just north of Mount Shasta. Later that week, the group climbed to its summit. By the end of September, they were on their way back north, taking a somewhat different route along the western shore of Upper Klamath Lake. Waldo arrived home at his farm outside Salem around the end of October.

By the end of his nearly four-month journey, Judge Waldo likely knew more about the topography of the Cascades than any living Oregonian. Over a decade, he had walked and ridden almost the entire future route of the Oregon Skyline Trail from Mount Jefferson to the California border. His intimate knowledge of the mountains would inform and inspire what was perhaps his most important achievement.

After returning to Salem, Waldo began his first session serving in the Oregon state legislature. He promptly introduced House Joint Memorial No. 8, asking Congress to set aside and forever reserve Oregon's Cascade Range, "extending twelve miles on each side, substantially, of the summit of the range."[73] In the memorial, Waldo noted that "the purity of its atmosphere, and healthfulness, and other attractions render it most desirable that it be set aside and kept free and open forever as a public reserve, park, and resort for the people of Oregon and of the United States."

In an article for *The Forester* journal, Waldo argued that the reserves were vital "for inspiration and our own true recreation."[74] Indeed, Waldo wrote that "the provision for the recreation of the people is now one of the established principles of municipal and civil government."[75] He felt that setting aside protected forest reserves for recreation was a necessity to ensure the "happiness, comfort and development" of Oregonians.

The reserves proposal also reflected Waldo's complex ideas about land management, formulated during his years exploring the mountains. He envisioned a program of collaborative control over the reserves shared between the state and federal governments. He advocated prohibiting most commercial activities and homesteading inside the reserves and implementing measures to limit the impact of railroads crossing through the protected areas. The bill also made allowances for dispersed resort areas for recreation, established under lease agreements with the government. Many of his ideas for managing the reserves were far ahead of their time and would be remarkably like the land-use constructs adopted decades later by the U.S. Forest Service.

A modified version of Waldo's memorial passed the House but died in the Senate due to pressure from influential grazing interests. Waldo was undeterred by the setback. Although he served only one term in the legislature, Waldo was just beginning his tireless campaign to protect the Cascades. To achieve that goal, he eventually joined forces with William Steel, advocating at the federal level for the creation of the Cascade Range Forest Reserve and a national park at Crater Lake.

## OTHER EARLY TRAVELERS ALONG THE SKYLINE

Judge Waldo may have been the first Oregonian to traverse the future route of the Skyline Trail, but others soon followed. One notable pair was Dee Wright and Henry Yelkus, who covered much of the same ground during the summer of 1891. Wright was born near Molalla, Oregon, in 1872 and grew up among the local Indigenous community.[76] Henry Yelkus was a member of the Molalla tribe, born in the early 1840s around Dickey Prairie, southeast of Molalla. His father was a tribal chief and a signatory of the land-cession treaties of the Kalapuya tribes in the Willamette Valley in 1851 and of the Willamette Valley Treaty negotiated in 1855.

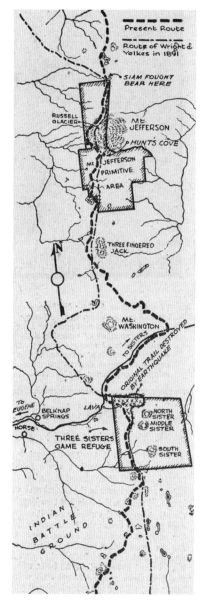

As a result of those treaties, the government forced Yelkus and members of his tribe to leave their homes and walk to Fort Yamhill, near the Grand Ronde Reservation.[77] When the government failed to meet its treaty obligations, Yelkus and his family returned to Dickey Prairie in the early 1860s. By then, many Euro-American settlers had moved into the area, dramatically altering the home they once knew.

Henry Yelkus established a homestead in the area and was on good terms with his neighbors, becoming a respected community member. There, he became friends with Dee Wright. In the summer of 1891, the two men set out for the Klamath Agency, planning to follow a route along the Cascade Crest. They started up the Molalla River, connecting to the crest trail around Breitenbush Lake. Yelkus was familiar with the route from previous travels and guided the

*Opposite*: Map of the 1930s Skyline Trail and the earlier route used by Henry Yelkes and Dee Wright during the summer of 1891. *The Sunday Oregonian* and the *Oregon Historical Society*.

*This page, top*: Henry Yelkes of the Molalla tribe, undated image. *U.S. Forest Service and the Oregon Historical Society*.

*This page, bottom*: Government packer Dee Wright on the summit of Mount Adams, September 1918. Together, Wright and Yelkes would travel much of the future Skyline route during the summer of 1891. *U.S. Forest Service and the Oregon Historical Society*.

young Dee Wright around Mount Jefferson, past Pamelia Lake and up into Hunts Cove before continuing over Minto Pass.

South of Three Fingered Jack, near Hogg Rock, the pair went to the west of the Belknap Crater lava field, between Twin Crater and Frog Camp, then continued south past the Three Sisters through Wickiup Plain. From Elk Lake, the men paralleled the later Skyline route, passing by Crane Prairie and Davis, Crescent and Fish Lakes, before turning east at Mount Thielsen toward the Klamath Agency. At the journey's end, Dee Wright asked his friend how long the trail had been there. Yelkus replied, "The trails of my people? Why, they have been here—always."[78]

The trip must have made a lasting impression on the young Dee Wright because he would spend the next forty years working the same routes as a government packer and trail builder for the Forest Service. He began his career around 1910, working around Mount Hood and later in the Willamette National Forest. Over the next twenty years, Wright helped build miles of trails and fire lookouts through the Cascades, including the summit fire lookout on the top of Mount Hood.

The Skyline Trail formed the bookends of Wright's life. Forty years after he and Henry Yelkus scouted a path through the lava fields west of Mount Washington, Wright was tasked with rerouting that section of the trail to improve the path for Skyline travelers. That assignment was his last project in the High Cascades. In the summer of 1934, Wright suffered a fatal heart attack while working as a foreman for a Civilian Conservation Corps crew that was rerouting the section of trail that he and Henry Yelkus had crossed as young men in 1891.

## Judge Waldo, William Steel and the Fight for the Cascade Range

Waldo's idea about creating a reserve along the Cascade Range emerged from his discussions with William Gladstone Steel, founder of the Mazamas, Oregon's famous mountaineering club. Steel was born in Ohio, and his family settled in Portland in the early 1870s. After a trip to Crater Lake in 1885, Steel became passionate about making the area a national park.

Two years later, Steel founded an outing group called the Oregon Alpine Club.[79] The club's roster included many prominent Oregonians, and Steel skillfully leveraged their influence to promote his campaign for

William Gladstone Steel was the founder of the Mazamas and played a pivotal role in establishing the Cascade Range Forest Reserve and Crater Lake National Park. *Oregon Historical Society.*

Crater Lake. Steel launched the effort at an opportune time. During the 1880s, there was a growing concern over waste and fraud on public lands across the West. A series of land scandals put pressure on politicians in Washington, D.C., to improve forest management practices and protect the public domain from exploitation.[80]

Waldo and Steel had very different personalities, but their talents were complementary. Waldo was shy, reserved and bookish. He avoided large crowds and seemed happiest on his long journeys into the Cascades.[81] Waldo's most potent weapons in the fight for the Cascades were his intellect and pen. He had unparalleled knowledge of the mountains and wrote eloquently in their defense.

In contrast, Steel was the gregarious public face of the campaign. His outgoing personality was well-suited to the public glad-handing and organizational aspects of the task. Steel's political savvy and persistence made him a perfect lobbyist to work the corridors of power in Salem and Washington, D.C. What united the men was their shared passion for the Cascade Range and a desire to protect it for future generations.

The men first discussed seeking federal protection for the range as early as 1886 when Steel began advocating for Crater Lake.[82] After Waldo's failed measure in the state legislature, their hopes were revived by the passage of the Forest Reserve Act signed by President Benjamin Harrison in 1891. The law revised previous legislation that had allowed land fraud and misuse of natural resources on public lands. The new act authorized the president to designate public lands as protected "forest reserves" and guard against exploitation.

Waldo and Steel recognized this as an opportunity to protect the lands along the Cascade Crest. Steel used his leverage with the Oregon Alpine Club to launch the campaign, while Waldo offered his legal expertise and intimate knowledge of the land under consideration. Their effort found support among many Oregonians and members of the state legislature at a time when there were growing concerns about protecting municipal water supplies originating in the Cascades.

Steel and the Oregon Alpine Club likely would have been satisfied with gaining several smaller reserves, but Waldo was adamant about preserving the entire range. In his correspondence with Steel, Waldo specifically mentioned Central Oregon's high lakes region, where he had spent many summers.[83] More than anyone, Waldo understood the necessity of preserving the range as an intact ecosystem rather than a patchwork of protected forests.[84]

A final decision on the reserve was delayed by the election of 1892 and the transition from defeated incumbent president Benjamin Harrison to incoming president Grover Cleveland. After the dust settled, Steel left for Washington to lobby for the reserve while Waldo embarked on his annual summer trip to the mountains. Waldo spent most of that trip exploring the area around Opal Lake, French Creek and Elk Lake, north of Detroit. He climbed several surrounding peaks and ended the excursion enjoying the waters at Breitenbush Hot Springs.[85]

After Waldo arrived home from his summer adventures, he received good news from Washington. On September 28, 1893, President Cleveland created the Cascade Range Forest Reserve by executive order, encompassing almost five million acres and making it the largest reserve in the nation. The area included a twenty-mile strip along the Cascade Crest, extending two hundred miles south from the Columbia River, including most of the future path of the Oregon Skyline Trail.

Steel and the Oregon Alpine Club had been the public faces of the campaign, but Waldo was its intellectual inspiration. Steel acknowledged as much in a letter published in *The Oregonian*, crediting Waldo's 1889 memorial to the state legislature as the idea's origin. Steel noted that Waldo was "more familiar with the summit of the range as a whole than any other man" and predicted that "future generations will see the wisdom of having reserved the tract."[86]

While the reserve had many backers, it also had enemies. Chief among them was the sheep lobby, which viewed the reserve as a potential threat to their grazing rights. At first, there was hope for a compromise allowing some livestock grazing within the reserve. However, the stakes were raised when the General Land Office, charged with managing the reserves, decided to prohibit grazing inside its boundaries.[87]

This decision sparked a fierce political campaign by the sheep lobby to have Oregon's congressional delegation pressure President Cleveland to reverse his executive order, thereby opening the range to grazing. As the threat reached a crisis point, Steel left for Washington, D.C., in early 1896 to save the reserve.

As Steel began his mission, Waldo sent his friend a flattering note of encouragement. He wrote that "the sheep men forgot one thing before they started in to murder the Cascade Mountains—they should have dispatched a man East, to assassinate you."[88] While Steel pressed their case in Washington, Waldo and supporters back in Oregon did their part with a letter-writing campaign and petitions.

Judge Waldo strategized with Steel on how to best fight the sheep men and aided the effort with an eloquent message to President Cleveland. It was something only Waldo could have written. In his magisterial letter, Waldo demonstrated his intimate knowledge of the region's natural history and his command of the complex political aspects concerning forest policy and grazing issues.

Waldo closed his letter with quotes from Emerson and Thoreau, adding a few thoughts about the importance of preserving the Cascades. He argued that men needed "not only fields to toil in, but mountains and wilderness to camp in, to hunt and fish…in communion with untrammeled nature."[89] Shortly after sending the letter, Waldo received assurances from his contacts in Washington that President Cleveland would take no action that might threaten the reserve.

Steel returned to Oregon victorious, then turned his attention to the campaign for establishing Crater Lake as a national park. Two years earlier, Steel had created a successor organization to the Oregon Alpine Club called the Mazamas. The new club's roster was filled with influential Oregonians ready to fight for the Cascades and Crater Lake.

In the summer of 1896, while on the Mazamas' annual club outing, Steel received an urgent request to escort members of the National Forest Commission on a fact-finding tour to Crater Lake. The commission's task was to report on the conditions of the western forest reserves and make recommendations to Congress and the president for their management.

The commission's membership included notable scientists and explorers. Among them were the famous naturalist John Muir and the future first chief of the Forest Service, Gifford Pinchot. Also on the trip was Henry Larcom Abbot, representing the Army Corps of Engineers. Abbot had led the Pacific Railroad Survey of 1855, the first expedition to explore and map interior portions of the High Cascades. Judge Waldo was in the area during the visit but, true to character, he avoided the official entourage and instead camped a few miles away at a quiet spot near Mount Scott.

After the trip, the commission recommended maintaining all existing forest reserves and adding additional reserves. President Cleveland acted on those recommendations the following year, creating thirteen new forest reserves. The commission also recommended eliminating grazing within the reserves, which reignited the fight in Oregon and other western states over how the land would be managed.[90]

The commission members supported turning Crater Lake into a national park.[91] Pinchot had been particularly impressed with the area during his visit, calling it "a wonder of the world."[92] In 1902, as head of the Division of Forestry under the Department of Agriculture, Pinchot helped push through the legislation that finally designated Crater Lake as a national park. Steel would later become the park's second superintendent in 1913 and was instrumental in developing the Crater Lake Lodge and the first Rim Road. He served as the park's commissioner from 1916 until he died in 1934.[93]

After the successful defense of the reserve in 1896, Waldo continued advocating for the protection of his beloved Cascades. Oregon's sheep men sustained their campaign to eliminate grazing restrictions inside the reserves. Waldo understood firsthand what unrestricted grazing did to the forests.

William Steel escorting Oregon senators John Mitchell and Charles Fulton, Governor George Chamberlain and the famed poet Joaquin Miller during a promotional tour of Crater Lake in 1903. *Oregon Historical Society.*

In the summer of 1896, he was back at Crane Prairie for the first time in thirteen years and startled to discover that "the wilderness is in great part gone that made it so attractive at the time."[94] The wild animals had left, giving the area entirely over to sheep.

This long-simmering controversy over grazing placed Waldo in direct opposition with his old friend John Minto, who had scouted many of the early trails between Mount Washington and Mount Jefferson. Minto had been a staunch advocate of the sheep industry since his days raising pure-bred Merino sheep in the Willamette Valley.

During the 1895–96 debate over the reserve's future, Minto had written numerous newspaper editorials supporting grazing.[95] As a spokesman for Oregon's woolgrowers, Minto had financial stakes in the debate, but he was also skeptical about the claims of the ecological damage caused by grazing. Furthermore, Minto was suspicious about federal control over Oregon's public lands and preferred a system of state-level forest management.[96]

Waldo also had to fend off attacks by business interests that wanted to lift use restrictions inside the reserves. A common theme ran through Waldo's battles against land speculators and the sheep men. He firmly believed that private commercial interests should not be allowed to exploit protected public lands. In a letter appearing in *The Forester* journal, Waldo argued that "mountain ranges, were nations wise, would never be permitted to become private property, but be kept the common property of all."[97]

*Left*: Oregon pioneer and politician John Minto helped establish a route over Santiam Pass and was a staunch defender of grazing rights in the Cascades. *Oregon Historical Society.*

*Below*: Sheep grazing in an alpine meadow near Three Fingered Jack, 1920. Photo by Myron Symons. *Oregon State University.*

Despite advancing age and faltering health, Waldo continued to make his annual summer outings into the High Cascades. In his final years, Waldo reflected on the changes that had occurred since he began exploring the Cascades nearly three decades earlier. In 1906, his travels took him up the Santiam River on his way to the mountains. While there, he noted that the "almost unbroken wilderness is no longer here" and the old solitudes were missing.[98]

In August 1907, Waldo began his final journey into the mountains. He traveled with a small group of friends, as he preferred. They planned to visit one of his favorite places in the Cascades near Mount Jefferson. The party made camp at Pamelia Lake and brought their horses to graze at the meadows in Hunts Cove. Waldo pushed himself to keep pace with the younger men in the group. When they decided to explore the upper slopes of Mount Jefferson, Waldo offered to guide them.

Waldo became ill from exertion during the climb and had to be carried out by stretcher to Detroit. His wife met him there a few days later and accompanied him back to their farm outside Salem. Waldo died there in early September at the age of sixty-three. In the days after his death, a tribute in the *Capital Journal* conveyed his lifelong love for the mountains, observing that "the forest was his temple, and there he worshipped."[99]

For twenty-seven summers, Waldo had journeyed to the mountains and left an enduring legacy as a protector of the Cascades. During those years, he covered virtually the entire route of what would become the Skyline Trail. More importantly, he became the driving force in establishing the Cascade Range Forest Reserve, providing a contiguous strip of protected forest along the mountain crest.

More than anyone, Waldo understood the importance of protecting the entire range to avoid having it "altogether cut up into cabbage patches."[100] Above all, he wanted to preserve these special places that could remain "undisturbed by human depredation."[101] It was his vision that enabled everything else that followed—including the Oregon Skyline Trail.

## Early Work of the General Land Office

By the late 1890s, Oregon's forest reserves were firmly established; however, these vast areas were virtually without management on the ground. In 1897, Congress passed the Organic Act, funding a small ranger force under the

General Land Office (GLO) tasked with supervising and protecting the reserves. Unfortunately, the higher-level superintendents and supervisors in the GLO were political appointees who often lacked experience in resource management and forestry.

The early GLO rangers working on the ground were not trained foresters but were experienced woodsmen familiar with their territory. They typically spent summer and autumn patrolling their districts. They had many responsibilities, including timber work, range inspections, enforcing land regulations, surveying, boundary work, fire spotting and trailblazing. Often, these rangers had to cover an enormous area of land, making it challenging to enforce rules and regulations.

Among the first cohort of rangers to work the reserves was Cy Bingham, who began his service in 1903. Bingham was born in Michigan and settled in Lane County around the turn of the century.[102] He was one of a handful of rangers responsible for patrolling the area of the Central Cascades between the Three Sisters and Crater Lake. During the winters, Cy and his wife, Connie, lived in McKenzie Bridge and Oakridge. During the summers, Connie often

Government Land Office ranger camp at Davis Lake, circa 1904. *Deschutes National Forest.*

joined Cy for extended periods while he worked in the mountains. He was also an amateur poet who often wrote verse during trail breaks.

One of Bingham's many responsibilities was locating and marking the trails through his jurisdiction. During the GLO era, the trails were created for administrative and logistical purposes rather than recreation. They were mainly used for land management functions and tasks such as firefighting. When Cy Bingham began patrolling the range in 1903, his routes were little more than faint footpaths through the forests made by Indigenous Oregonians, sheep herders and miners. There were few permanent structures and almost no amenities along the crest.[103]

Before 1910, the government had no accurate maps depicting the interior of the High Cascades. Bingham was among the first rangers to mark and number the informal trails along the central and southern ranges. He did this using a series of tree carvings along the route. Bingham's trail markings served several purposes. They were a record of his travels, aids for navigation and markers for designating grazing rights. To make his trail markings, Bingham would chop off a section of bark and then carve his name, date and a trail number into the tree, guiding others using the trail.

During his first season in the reserve, Bingham built a ranger cabin at Crescent Lake and blazed a trail to Davis Lake. He also helped cut a route to the top of Maiden Peak, rising above Willamette Pass. The site was later used as a fire lookout.[104] The following summer, Bingham built another cabin at Crane Prairie. He also surveyed sites for future resorts and camps as early visitors began exploring the forests for recreation.

In 1905, Bingham and the other rangers were transferred from the GLO to the newly created Forest Service. With the new bureaucratic structure, rangers received a "use book" outlining their duties and responsibilities. That summer, Bingham received an assignment to mark out a trail from McKenzie Bridge to Crater Lake, blazing a large section of the route that would become the Skyline Trail.[105] It took him two summers to complete the entire circuit, leaving a trail of marked "Bingham Trees" along his route.

The exact number of Bingham Trees along that section of the Skyline route is unknown. He claimed to have lost count after thirty, so there were likely many more.[106] By the 1970s, around two dozen of the marked trees were still standing. Many of these were clustered between Cowhorn Mountain and Waldo Lake. But some were found as far north as Separation Meadow in the Three Sisters Wilderness.

In total, Bingham spent five years working along the Cascade Crest. During that time, he and Connie firmly established the future route of the

*This page*: Government Land Office ranger Cy Bingham worked along the future Skyline route with his wife, Connie, from 1903 to 1907. *U.S. Forest Service.*

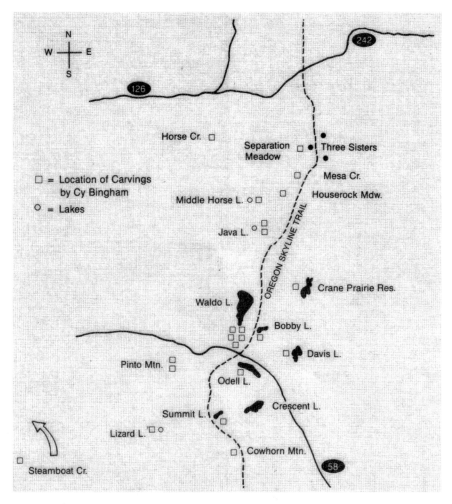

Map of known "Bingham trees" along the Skyline Trail route, catalogued by Robert Cox starting in the late 1960s. Robert Cox, *Blazes on the Skyline*.

Skyline Trail, blazing the way for others to follow. In November 1907, he was named forest supervisor of the newly created Malheur National Forest, based out of John Day. He served in that position until 1920, when he was elected sheriff of Grant County. Bingham later recalled his days in the Cascades as "the best five years of my life."[107]

Sixty years later, a retired barber and hiker from Eugene named Robert Cox embarked on a twenty-year mission to locate and map the remaining Bingham Trees. Cox painstakingly tracked down and documented every known carving and later published a book on his findings.[108] The result

One of the few remaining Cy Bingham trees on display in the Deschutes County Museum. Photo by author. *Courtesy of the Deschutes County Historical Society.*

was a detailed record of Bingham's travels during those years. Based on that record, Cox considered Bingham the "Father of the Skyline Trail" for his contributions in blazing its eventual path. In 1920, when the Skyline Trail was formally mapped, the survey team noted the presence of several Bingham Trees along the route.[109]

Bingham's time on the trail ended with a symbolic coda in 1924 when he returned to one of his old camps at Odell Lake. He was shocked to find the place filled with cars and people recreating around the lake. In a poem, Bingham lamented the "autos parked where once we tied our horses to the trees."[110] He observed with regret how cars had "widened out the old pack trail over which the autos spin, that I once built from the Sisters, south clear to the crater rim."

## ESTABLISHMENT OF THE FOREST SERVICE AND NEW PRIORITIES

Rangers like Cy Bingham did difficult and admirable work with few resources. However, many viewed the General Land Office with suspicion. Waldo and Steel considered its higher-level management an outright threat to the forest reserves.[111] A series of land fraud cases in the early part of the century only reinforced suspicions that the land office could not be trusted.[112]

By that time, Gifford Pinchot was serving as head of the Division of Forestry within the Department of Agriculture before that office became the U.S. Forest Service. In that role, he pushed to professionalize forest administration. With the support of his friend President Theodore Roosevelt, Pinchot achieved a major bureaucratic restructuring in 1905. Under the plan, the forest reserves were transferred from the GLO under the Department of the Interior to Pinchot's control under the Department of Agriculture.

As part of the change, the old Bureau of Forestry was replaced by a newly formed agency known as the Forest Service, led by Pinchot. He soon ended the system of political appointments and reformed the hiring system. From then on, new foresters had to take comprehensive field tests and pass a written civil service examination.

With the creation of the Forest Service, the Cascade Range Forest Reserve was redesignated as the Cascade National Forest in 1907. The following year, it was divided into the Oregon, Cascade, Umpqua and Crater National Forests. Eventually, the original area of the reserve would encompass the modern footprints of the Mount Hood, Willamette, Umpqua and Rogue River National Forests, along with parts of the Deschutes and Winema National Forests.

When the Forest Service took over management of the reserves, its initial focus was on resource management. The agency's priorities under Pinchot were range administration, timber sales, fire control, grazing and game management. During the first decade, recreation received little attention and no funding. However, the newly created Forest Service continued to scout and develop a system of trails running along the Cascade Crest.

In 1910, the supervisor of the Willamette National Forest developed a proposal for creating a network of trails stretching from Mount Hood to Crater Lake. The plan called for a series of central and branch trails connected at junctions no more than twenty miles apart. The standard trail width was twelve inches wide, the tread of a horse, with a grade of no more than 10 percent. Ranger stations would be established at intervals along the trails. Over the next decade, the Forest Service built around 450 miles of such trails around the state.[113]

However, these early trails through the Cascades were not developed with recreation in mind. The Forest Service used them primarily for ranger duties such as surveying, inspecting land claims, timber management, patrolling and overseeing grazing permits. But by the turn of the century, more Oregonians were using the national forests for pleasure and recreation. Early outdoor clubs like the Mazamas were frequent visitors to the forests and used the trails for hiking, camping and accessing climbing objectives. By the start of the 1920s, recreational use of the national forest trail systems had increased dramatically.

## From Wagon Roads to Scenic Highways: The Opening of the Cascades

An important catalyst drawing Oregonians into the national forests was access to automobiles. Cars began appearing on Oregon roads shortly after the turn of the century. In 1903, John Kelly became the first to drive an automobile from Portland to Government Camp.[114] In 1905, a car named "Old Steady" was the first to travel over Santiam Pass as part of a transcontinental race for the Lewis and Clark Centennial Exposition in Portland.[115] Henry Ford began the initial production of the Model T a few years later in 1908, bringing automobile ownership within reach of middle-class Americans. By 1911, the first automobile had completed the route over Willamette Pass.[116] Although these routes were still primitive roads, they offered Oregonians a much easier way of accessing the High Cascades for leisure and recreation.

Given the growing popularity of automobiles, Oregon lawmakers in 1913 created the State Highway Commission to help improve the region's roads. The commission's simple mandate was to "get Oregon out of the mud." At the time, there were only a few miles of paved roads outside the state's urban areas. But that number would increase dramatically in the coming decade as the Good Roads Movement advocated for increased spending on rural byways, greatly improving access to the national forests. Economic development, auto tourism and outdoor recreation became inextricably linked in the minds of state officials and the Forest Service.[117]

During the same period, the American Automobile Association unveiled its "See American First" campaign, encouraging domestic tourism by car. The newly established National Park Service was quick to embrace this new trend of auto tourism. Crater Lake was one of the first parks to welcome automobile visits starting in 1911. Construction of the Rim Road began two years later, and by 1917 the park offered its first automobile guide map for

A time of transition. One of the last wagons to cross the old Santiam Pass Road, circa 1910. *U.S. Forest Service.*

visitors touring the lake by car.[118] But the era's signature roadbuilding effort was the Columbia River Highway, which started in 1913.

Seattle engineer Samuel Lancaster was closely involved in the road's design and construction. Lancaster had studied the great scenic roads of Europe and intended to create something of equivalent stature along the Columbia River. He planned the route with this goal in mind, highlighting "where the most beautiful things along the line might be seen to the best advantage."[119] Lancaster painstakingly studied the terrain and located the bridges, tunnels and overlooks to maximize dramatic views of the gorge. When completed, the route was one of the first paved highways in the Pacific Northwest and considered America's first scenic highway.[120]

Perhaps more than any other project, the Columbia River Highway demonstrated the overlapping interests among good roads advocates, tourism promotors, and the Forest Service. The project reflected a central belief that roads, recreation and economic development went hand in hand.[121] The prominent Seattle railroad executive and good roads advocate Samuel Hill was a major supporter of the Columbia River Highway and saw the road's

"Old Steady" was one of the first automobiles to travel over Santiam Pass during the "Hell Gate to Portland" transcontinental race in 1905. *U.S. Forest Service.*

value in terms of aesthetics and profit. Of the road's potential, he predicted, "We will cash in, year after year, on our crop of scenic beauty, without depleting it in any way."[122]

The initial segment of road from Portland to Hood River opened in 1915. That same year, the Forest Service set aside fourteen thousand acres along the route and designated it for recreation. When America's chief forester, Henry Graves, toured the new road, he said he didn't know "anywhere in the world where so many wonderful things are crowded into such a short distance as along the Columbia River Highway."[123] The following year, the Forest Service approved the initial plan for the Mount Hood Loop Road. Both projects became enormous catalysts for auto-based outdoor recreation, putting day trips to Mount Hood within easy reach of Portlanders.

When the Eagle Creek Campground along the Columbia River Highway opened in 1916, it became the nation's first modern campground designed for automobile camping. The site offered campsites with concrete stoves, picnic tables and outhouses, situated around individual parking spots. In

The early days of auto tourism. Driving along the rim of Crater Lake. *Oregon Historical Society.*

Sightseeing along the Mount Hood Loop Highway during the early 1920s. *U.S. Forest Service.*

*Above*: The welcome kiosk at the Eagle Creek Campground in the Columbia River Gorge National Scenic Area, 1916. *U.S. Forest Service.*

*Opposite*: Early auto camping in Oregon's national forests, circa early 1930s. *U.S. Forest Service.*

the first season, Eagle Creek attracted some fifteen thousand visitors and became the Forest Service's prototype design for campgrounds in the new era of auto tourism.[124]

When Eagle Creek opened, there was one automobile for every 13 residents of Multnomah County. Just over a decade later, 1 of every 3.7 residents owned an automobile.[125] With improved infrastructure and rising car ownership, recreational visits to the national forests quadrupled between 1917 and 1924.[126] By the early 1920s, Mount Hood National Forest was one of the most visited spots in the entire National Forest System. In response to surging demand, the Forest Service began developing more recreational areas and campgrounds, primarily geared toward auto tourism.

With work underway on the Mount Hood Loop and Crater Lake Rim Road, there was significant enthusiasm for constructing other scenic highways around the state. An editorial in *The Oregonian* boasted that the state was so blessed with natural beauty that "it was impossible to build a highway without it becoming a scenic road."[127] Thus, when Oregon's state park system was established in 1921, it was organized under the State Highway

Commission with a mandate to preserve scenic beauty along highways and provide for roadside parks and attractions.[128]

Within this context, the Forest Service conceived an idea to build a grand scenic highway along the backbone of the Cascades. The plan was formally announced in the pages of *The Oregonian* on January 1, 1920, under the banner headline, "Proposed Skyline Road Through the Cascades' Grandeur Is Held Practical."[129]

The proposed route would leave Government Camp, passing by Clear and Olallie Lakes. From there, it would circle west around Mount Jefferson, past Marion Lake and Three Fingered Jack, continuing west of Mount Washington before crossing McKenzie Road near Frog Camp. After tracking along the western slopes of the Three Sisters, the route would cross Wickiup Plain, then skirt Sparks, Elk, Lava and Cultus Lakes before crossing back over the crest around Irish Lake and hugging the eastern shoreline of Waldo Lake. The road would then return over the divide south of Maiden Peak and pass along the shores of Odell and Crescent Lakes before continuing to Diamond Lake and Mount Thielsen, finally ending at Crater Lake.

The article described the ongoing work to improve the main lateral routes linking Oregon's population centers to the proposed Skyline Road. These routes included the Mount Hood Loop Road, the Santiam and McKenzie highways and a new road between Medford and Klamath Falls crossing the mountains at Crater Lake. The article prophesized that "the Oregon

Skyline, with its lateral roads, will make the glories of the Cascades available to autoists and bring them nearer to the town dwellers."[130]

In addition to opening spectacular scenery, the article touted the road's enormous economic potential, first as a tourist attraction but also as a means for accessing the vast forest resources trapped deep inside the rugged interior of the Cascades. The article also cited the road's utility as a logistical network for firefighting, enabling the construction of remote airfields to support airborne fire patrols. Another benefit of the road would be accessing previously unreachable timber stands and grazing areas, "overcoming the barrier of the high mountain range and bringing the market nearer to the producer."[131]

The article predicted that the proposed Skyline Road "unquestionably will be an enormous asset to the state and develop a tremendous playground for all America," becoming one of the "greatest scenic drives" in the country.[132] Six months later, forester Frederick Cleator departed from Crater Lake to begin a four-month reconnaissance to survey and map the proposed route.

## 3

# CHANGES ON THE LAND

## *The Forest Service, Conservation and Outdoor Recreation*

The idea of outdoor recreation began gaining popularity in America in the late nineteenth century. These early activities mostly revolved around traditional outdoor pursuits like hunting, fishing and camping but also included hiking and mountaineering. At the time, they were considered elite pursuits, available only to those with money, leisure time and access to the wilderness. But by the early twentieth century, outdoor recreation was becoming more accessible to the masses and promoted as a healthy escape from the confinements of urban living.[133]

On the East Coast, early outdoor clubs had formed in the decades after the Civil War, including groups such as the White Mountain Club and Appalachian Mountain Club. On the West Coast, similar clubs began forming in the 1890s, including the Sierra Club, the Mountaineers of Seattle and the Mazamas of Portland. Many of these clubs mixed recreation with scientific exploration and conservation efforts.

When the Mazamas formed in 1894, it became one of the nation's earliest mountaineering societies. It was composed primarily of middle-class professionals, with many women among the charter members.[134] Its roster included influential Portland business and political leaders active in William Steel's efforts to protect Crater Lake and the Cascade Range Forest Reserve.

The club played an essential role in documenting Oregon's early mountaineering history by establishing summit register boxes on the state's notable peaks.[135] The club kept detailed records of its activities through newsletters, annual reports and scientific studies. In the early twentieth

Mazama hikers on the trail to Jefferson Park, 1907. *Mazama Library and Historical Collection.*

century, Mazama-sponsored studies provided some of the most detailed information available on the geology and ecology of the Cascades.

The club's roster included many highly experienced climbers, but Steel also encouraged novices to learn and experience the mountains. He was an enthusiastic promoter of outdoor recreation for the average person and determined to make the mountains accessible to anyone.[136] Steel's desire to popularize outdoor recreation extended into his later role as the superintendent at Crater Lake, where he worked to expand access and visitation to the park.

Mazama outings into the Cascades played a central role in popularizing hiking and climbing in Oregon. The group was known for its annual trips to the mountains, where participants could enjoy the natural surroundings while climbing and hiking. Through such trips, the Mazamas became some of the most active early users of the Skyline route, even before the trail was formally established in the 1920s.

The Mazamas frequented the slopes of Mount Hood but also made expeditions to the Central and Southern Cascades. On these trips, they often used sections of the future Skyline route to access their base camps and climbing objectives. The club made its first annual outing to the Three Sisters region in 1903, making their camp near the Obsidian Cliffs on the western side of North Sister. During that trip, they placed registry boxes on the top of the South Sister and Middle Sister.[137]

The next outing to Central Oregon came in 1910, based out of Frog Camp. On that trip, club members summited all Three Sisters, Broken Top, Bachelor Butte and the Husband. The outing also produced a detailed physiographic study of the central Cascade region. The Mazamas returned to the area again in 1916. That trip included many non-climbers who enjoyed day hikes from Camp Riley along the Skyline route to the west of the Three Sisters. That encampment produced a detailed assessment of the region's glaciers.[138] The club also made annual outings to the Mount Jefferson region in 1900, 1907 and 1917.

After Frederick Cleator's 1920 Skyline survey, the Mazamas continued their trips along the trail. In the summer of 1921, a group of sixty Mazamas covered the southern portion of the Skyline Trail, spending two weeks hiking from Crescent Lake to Crater Lake.[139] A newspaper account of the trip noted a telling change in how the Mazamas supported the trip. That year, the group used automobiles rather than packhorses to transport their equipment between the overnight stops along the trail.[140]

The Mazamas during an outing along the future Skyline route in the Three Sisters wilderness, circa 1910. *Mazama Library and Historical Collection.*

Another Mazama outing that summer covered a different section of the Skyline route between Mount Washington and Elk Lake. The trip report noted that the party had used Cleator's recently published Skyline Trail map for navigation.[141] By the time the Forest Service formally established the route in the early 1920s, few Oregonians had spent as much time along the Skyline route as the Mazamas.

## THE FOREST SERVICE SLOWLY EMBRACES OUTDOOR RECREATION

The Mazamas had been hiking and climbing in the High Cascades for years before the Forest Service fully embraced recreation as one of its core functions. As its role in recreation expanded, the agency maintained close informal ties with outdoor clubs like the Mazamas, the Skyliners of Bend and the Obsidians of Eugene. Many Forest Service personnel were club members and often helped plan group outings.[142]

The close relationship between the Forest Service and the outdoor groups was mutually beneficial. The clubs could obtain leases to build their cabins and other facilities on National Forest System lands. Meanwhile, the clubs helped the Forest Service with tasks such as trail building, scientific studies and performing search and rescue inside the national forests.

During the General Land Office era, no formal policy for managing recreation on public lands existed.[143] At first, there was little change as the Forest Service took over management of the reserves in 1905. Chief forester Gifford Pinchot was not opposed to recreation, per se, but had other priorities as he established the new agency. The Forest Service had no mandate or budget to support recreation during his tenure.[144]

The agency's perspective on recreation gradually shifted when Henry Graves took over as chief forester in 1910. Graves had previously helped establish the forestry graduate program at Yale University in 1900, the first of its kind in the United States. As he began his tenure as chief forester, Graves noted an increasing number of people using National Forest System lands for recreation, primarily hunting, fishing and camping.[145] In 1912, the Forest Service began compiling statistics on recreation. That year, an estimated 1.5 million visitors used national forest lands for recreational day visits, while around 230,000 people stayed overnight for camping.[146]

In 1921, the agency's annual report observed that "with the construction of new roads and trails, the forests are visited more and more for recreation purposes, and in consequence, the demand is growing rapidly for sites on which summer camps, cottages, and hotels may be located."[147] The following year, Graves acknowledged that recreation was becoming a "highly important use of the Forests by the public." In some cases, he suggested, recreation should even take priority over commercial use of the forests.[148] That statement reflected a significant shift in how the agency viewed recreation within the context of its traditional land management functions.

In many respects, Oregon was at the forefront of this transition. With national forests comprising 25 percent of the state's land area, most Oregonians were only a short drive from recreational opportunities on public lands. By 1920, Mount Hood was one of the busiest recreational areas in the entire country. But the surging number of visitors also raised concerns over sanitation, safety and fire risk. The Forest Service had to quickly develop policies for dealing with changes on the ground.

*Left*: A group of Skyline Trail travelers in the early 1920s at the Lemiti Ranger Station on the Mount Hood National Forest. *U.S. Forest Service.*

*Below*: A view from the Mount Hood Loop Road, 1925. *Oregon State University.*

In 1912, the Columbia and Oregon National Forests (later the Gifford Pinchot and Mount Hood National Forests) produced the agency's first maps specifically designed for recreational visitors.[149] By the mid-1920s, such maps were becoming commonplace. In 1915, the Forest Service published its first handbook for campers, providing rules, regulations and practical tips on camping in the national forests. The following year, the Forest Service opened its first auto campground at Eagle Creek along the Columbia River Highway within what was then called the Oregon National Forest.

With surging interest in outdoor recreation, the Forest Service hired Professor Frank Waugh, one of the country's leading landscape architects, to survey recreation in the national forests. Some of the motivation driving the survey was likely related to a sense of competition with the new National Park Service. During the early years, there was bureaucratic rivalry between the two agencies concerning control over the nation's most scenic recreational lands.[150]

Waugh spent five months touring the country and published his report, titled *Recreation Use on the National Forests*, the following year. In the report, Waugh observed that recreational activities on forest lands had "multiplied and intensified," placing them on par with traditional forest uses like timber production and grazing.[151] He noted the automobile's impact on recreation patterns, providing citizens with a new way to access the outdoors. Waugh cited the Columbia River Highway and the Eagle Creek Campground as examples of the rising popularity of auto-based outdoor recreation.[152]

In 1918, Waugh authored another influential report titled *Landscape Engineering in the National Forests*.[153] The report considered the challenges of designing landscapes for outdoor recreation, such as campgrounds and scenic trails. Waugh's writings on the topic significantly influenced Frederick Cleator when he scouted the route for the proposed Skyline Road.[154] After the reconnaissance, Cleator corresponded with Waugh about his work on the project.

Waugh was one of the first to argue that the Forest Service should view recreation as a primary use of National Forest System lands, placing it on par with traditional resource management functions. While some in the agency were reluctant to embrace recreation, others worried that the Forest Service was going too far in promoting recreational development. One of those critics was Aldo Leopold, considered by some to be the "Father of the National Forest Wilderness System."[155]

Leopold was a forester and naturalist, perhaps best known for his 1949 book, *A Sand County Almanac*. Leopold began his career with the Forest Service around the same time as Frederick Cleator, among the initial cohort of professional foresters brought into the agency by Gifford Pinchot. During his early years with the Forest Service, Leopold worked primarily in Arizona and New Mexico. In the early 1900s, he developed the agency's first comprehensive management plan for the Grand Canyon before it became a national park. He later helped establish the Gila Wilderness Area, the agency's first designated wilderness area. However, Leopold gradually became dismayed with how the Forest Service was promoting roadbuilding and infrastructure development on system lands.[156]

In 1921, Leopold wrote an influential article in the *Journal of Forestry* in which he defined his concept of wilderness as "a continuous stretch of

*Above*: Aldo Leopold on his horse Polly on the Carson National Forest, New Mexico, 1911. *University of Wisconsin–Madison Archives.*

*Right*: Aldo Leopold, 1928. *University of Wisconsin–Madison Archives.*

country preserved in its natural state, open to lawful hunting and fishing, big enough to absorb a two weeks' pack trip."[157] Leopold wanted to ensure that some areas within the national forest system could be left "devoid of roads, artificial trails, cottages, or other works of man."[158] As his concept of "wilderness" matured in subsequent decades, he came to view it as defined recreational space without development.

The tension between Leopold's understanding of "wilderness" and the vision for the proposed Skyline Road reflected two conflicting schools of thought about how the Forest Service approached recreational development. In many respects, the Skyline Road proposal represented everything that Leopold was against—roadbuilding, auto-based recreation, and the commercialization of nature.

To some degree, Frederick Cleator represented the opposite side of the spectrum. Before embarking on the Skyline Road project, Cleator played a central role in developing residential cabins, recreational resorts and campgrounds on national forest lands throughout the Cascades. Conversely, Leopold was advocating for wilderness areas defined by the absence of such things. Over time, both philosophical visions would profoundly influence how the Oregon Skyline Trail evolved.

## Frederick Cleator and Oregon's Outdoor Recreation Infrastructure

As recreation became an increasingly significant part of the Forest Service's mission, the agency developed policies encouraging the development of recreational infrastructure. In 1915, Congress passed the Term Permit Act, expanding the scope and duration of recreational permitting in the national forests. This act enabled the development of summer homes, private camps, resorts, and hotels inside the national forests.

In 1916, the Deschutes National Forest issued its first permits for recreational cabins along the Metolius River, followed by similar development on Elk, Odell and Paulina Lakes. At the same time, the agency was moving ahead on recreational residences around Mount Hood, including tracts around Zig-Zag, Camp Creek, Still Creek and Mile Bridge. By the 1920s, similar tracts were being developed at other locations along the Cascades, such as Breitenbush Hot Springs, along the McKenzie River, at Odell and Crescent Lakes and along Union Creek.

Tourists at the Union Creek resort, 1928. Forester Frederick Cleator helped plan the recreational facilities at Union Creek and stopped there during his 1920 Skyline survey to assess their progress. *U.S. Forest Service.*

A critical factor encouraging enthusiasm for outdoor recreation was the explosive growth of road and trail building inside the National Forests. In 1916, Congress passed the Rural Post Roads Act, providing federal funding and support for the construction of Forest Roads on public lands. This provision sparked a surge of trail-building and road development across Oregon. By 1932, the Forest Service had constructed 49 forest highways covering 1,372 miles inside Oregon's national forests.[159]

These roadbuilding initiatives brought many new recreational users to the nation's forests. Between 1917 and 1924, there was a fourfold increase in national forest visitation.[160] During the same time, there was enormous growth in the number of developed campgrounds inside the forests, increasing from 138 in 1920 to more than 1,700 by 1930.[161] By 1922, over one million people each year were using Forest Service campgrounds, up from around 200,000 just a decade earlier.[162]

As the Forest Service gradually embraced its new role of managing recreation, Frederick Cleator was at the forefront of that transition. Born in Minneapolis in 1883, Cleator later worked in Alaska and attended the

University of Minnesota. But before finishing his studies, he took the civil service exam to join the newly created Forest Service.

During the summer of 1908, Cleator came to Oregon and worked as a logger. When he received word that he had passed his civil service exam, he accepted a position with the Forest Service and reported for training in Wenatchee, Washington. The following year, Cleator began his career doing boundary work between the Chelan and Wenatchee National Forests.[163] Over the next decade, he worked as a ranger in various locations across Oregon and Washington.

As his career progressed, Cleator recognized that the Forest Service needed to move faster in response to the enormous growth of recreation on system lands. He was concerned that unless recreation was adequately regulated and managed, it would have detrimental impacts on the forests.[164] In Cleator's mind, this meant developing planned facilities and infrastructure specifically designed for recreational users.

Cleator's career path took a critical turn when he was transferred to the agency's district office in Portland, later called the Pacific Northwest Regional Office. There, he was given the title of "Recreation Examiner."[165] At the time, Cleator was one of only three Forest Service employees working specifically on recreation planning.[166] In that role, he developed much of the Pacific Northwest's recreational infrastructure during the 1920s and 1930s.

One of Cleator's primary responsibilities was managing the recreational residence program, which evolved from the 1915 Occupancy Permits Act. The law allowed for the development of recreation residences, summer camps, stores, hotels or other facilities on national forest lands with leases of up to thirty years.[167] Under the program, recreational residences were intended to be primitive, seasonal structures rather than year-round homes. They were built in rustic style, often using local stone and timber. The first tract of such cabins in the state began development in 1916 along the Metolius River, across from Camp Sherman.[168]

By the 1920s, the recreational residence program had become very popular with the public, and the Forest Service viewed it as a productive way to promote and manage recreation on system lands. Cleator was one of the program's leading advocates and personally oversaw the development of campgrounds and recreational residences at Government Camp, Odell and Elk Lakes, along the Metolius River tract, at Union Creek and the Oregon Caves, among other locations around the state.[169]

## A PLAN FOR THE SKYLINE ROAD

Cleator was working on the recreational residence program at the district office in Portland when he was tasked to survey a route for the Skyline Road over the summer of 1920. The Forest Service had begun its initial planning during the previous summer. However, the idea may have originated years earlier from an article in the *Oregon Journal* written by Lewis A. McArthur.

McArthur, known as "Tam," was one of the first Pacific Power and Light Company employees. In 1914, he was appointed to the Oregon Geographic Board and elected board secretary two years later. In this capacity, McArthur became the state's foremost authority on geographic place names and eventually published three editions of *Oregon Geographic Names*, the authoritative source on the state's place names.

In his 1915 article, McArthur suggested the construction of "a passable wagon road on or near the summit of the Cascade Range from the Columbia River to the California line."[170] McArthur's argument for the road, later echoed by other boosters, cited its scenic values and practical uses for firefighting and military functions. He noted that such a road would "open an almost incomparable storehouse of magnificent scenery of the most varied type." McArthur's suggestion must have resonated with leaders at the Oregon State Highway Commission. The following year, a provisional route for a secondary highway along the Cascade Crest appeared on a map presented to the state legislature depicting proposed state highway projects.[171]

Within a few years of McArthur's article, the Forest Service began exploring the possibility of such a road. Cleator later explained that much of the initial support for the project came from civic leaders hoping to promote Oregon tourism.[172] Influential boosters, including the State Chamber of Commerce and the Oregon State Motor Association, eagerly backed McArthur's idea. Their support for the ambitious proposal evolved within the context of two other major roadbuilding projects: the Columbia River Highway and the Mount Hood Loop Road.

By the summer of 1919, the Forest Service began actively exploring the possibility of turning existing trail segments along the Cascade Crest into a scenic highway. At the time, the southern section of the route between Santiam Pass and Crater Lake was relatively well-established. Judge Waldo, Cy Bingham and others had thoroughly scouted and marked much of that segment between 1890 and 1910.

The northern section of the route from Government Camp to Clackamas Lake was also well-established, following the path of an existing forest road passing by Clear Lake, Frog Lake and Summit Butte. T.M. Davis, an engineer with the Bureau of Public Roads, had previously surveyed that section.[173] However, the areas west of the Warms Springs Reservation and around Mount Jefferson were more remote and less well-traveled. The Forest Service decided to begin the survey along that section of the route.

In 1919, the Forest Service sent surveyor Kirk Cecil and the legendary Mount Hood guide Elijah "Lige" Coalman on a mission to blaze a route around Mount Jefferson.[174] At the time, there was a primitive trail leading into Jefferson Park from Detroit and another poorly marked path starting from Breitenbush Lake. The Forest Service wanted to improve access to Jefferson Park and use the new trail segment to close a gap in the proposed route for the Skyline Road.[175]

Few people were more well-qualified for the task than Cecil and Coalman. Cecil had begun his career as a forest guard in Montana. During World War I, he served as an officer in the coastal artillery corps stationed overseas.[176] After the war, he returned to the Forest Service, working as a roads and trails inspector, doing extensive surveying work in the Deschutes, Umpqua and Siskiyou National Forests. Cecil would later become supervisor of the Umatilla and Gifford Pinchot National Forests.

Elijah "Lige" Coalman (*left*) carrying supplies to the summit lookout on Mount Hood. *U.S. Forest Service.*

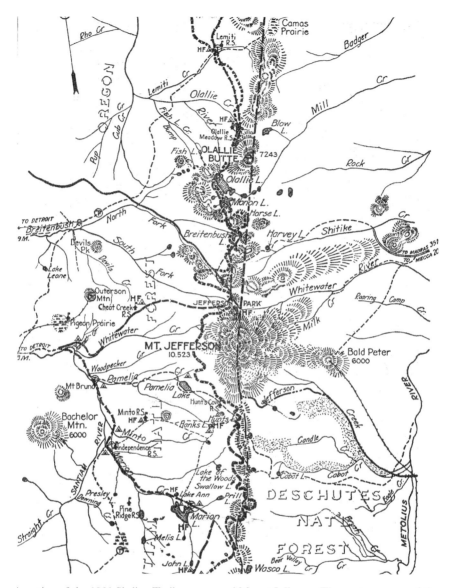

A section of the 1921 Skyline Trail map around Mount Jefferson. The route was one of the more remote sections of trail when Kirk Cecil and Lige Coalman blazed the path during the summer of 1919. *Oregon Historical Society.*

Cecil's partner in the trail scouting mission was Lige Coalman, a legendary mountaineer and rescuer who made his first ascent of Mount Hood at age sixteen, guided by his climbing mentor Oliver Yocum.[177] In the summer of 1915, while working for the Forest Service, Coalman built the fire lookout cabin on the top of Mount Hood. He hauled most of the supplies up the mountain with the assistance of government packer Dee Wright. After completing the summit cabin, Coalman became the first lookout during the summer of 1916.

Coalman summited Mount Hood nearly six hundred times during his career. But in 1918, he was severely injured in a rockfall on Cooper Spur, a glacial moraine extending northeast from the summit. Coalman struggled back to the summit and spent the night there before being carried down by a rescue party the next day.[178] By the following summer, he had recovered enough to lead the trail survey around Mount Jefferson.

Cecil and Coalman spent a month in the field scouting a route from Breitenbush Lake around the west side of Mount Jefferson. The Breitenbush area was still accessible only by trail until the road was built in the mid-1920s. Their path around Jefferson skirted east of Pamelia Lake before rejoining the ridgeline above Hunts Cove, then continued south along the crest to Minto Pass. The trail segment Cecil and Coalman blazed that summer would add a critical missing link to the proposed Skyline Road route. Cleator's party would cover much of the remaining ground between Mount Jefferson and Crater Lake the following summer.

## THE SKYLINE ROAD COMES INTO THE SPOTLIGHT

As Cecil and Coalman did their work in near obscurity, one of Oregon's most famous photographers, Fred Kiser, was also on the trail that summer. Kiser was born in Nebraska and moved to Portland as a child. As a young man, he became interested in photography and opened a studio in Portland with his brother.

Kiser was an avid outdoorsman, mountain climber, Mazama member and friend of William Steel. Through his relationship with Steel, Kiser began taking pictures around Crater Lake and the High Cascades. In 1903, Kiser accompanied Steele to Crater Lake as the photographer on a highly publicized promotional tour celebrating the newly created national park. Kiser got a career breakthrough two years later when he was selected as the official photographer of the 1905 Lewis and Clark Centennial Exhibition in Portland.[179]

Over the next few decades, Kiser became one of the era's most successful commercial photographers, widely known for his iconic landscape images

A Fred Kiser photograph taken during his trip along the Skyline route, circa 1918. *Willamette Falls & Landings Heritage Area Coalition.*

around the West. Kiser is credited with introducing sites like Crater Lake and the Columbia River Gorge to a national audience. In 1921, he was awarded the photo concession to work inside Crater Lake National Park, where his company performed photography services for visiting tourists.

Kiser specialized in nature photography and dramatic mountaineering images. Starting in 1903, his company served as the official photographer for the Mazamas' annual climbing trips. In this capacity, Kiser captured some of the earliest professional images along the Skyline route. He became known for his colorized stereoscopic photos and used these to promote roadbuilding projects such as the Columbia Gorge Highway, the Mount Hood Loop and later the Skyline Road.[180]

In 1919, at the height of his popularity, Kiser embarked on a one-month trip between Mount Hood and Crater Lake, taking photographs and promoting the idea for the tourist road along the Cascade Crest.[181] A small crew helped carry his photography equipment and camping gear. Kiser was joined by a businessman from Ohio who was writing an article about the Cascades for *National Geographic* magazine.[182]

Kiser took hundreds of photographs and five thousand feet of moving picture film during the journey. He later used the images to promote the Skyline Road, as well as a separate proposal for turning sections of the Cascade Crest into a national park. While neither the park nor the road ever materialized, Kiser is credited with popularizing the idea of building a scenic highway along the Cascade Crest. He became an early and enthusiastic promotor, believing that the Skyline Road would become "one of the most wonderful scenic highways in the world."

# 4

# MAPPING THE SKYLINE

## *Frederick Cleator's 1920 Reconnaissance*

Cleator was already very involved with the Forest Service's fledgling outdoor recreation program when he moved to the district office in Portland. While in Washington State, he led the early recreational surveys on what was then the Rainier National Forest, developing campgrounds and summer residence plans. In Portland, he began writing recreational pamphlets and visitor information guides. Given Cleator's background in recreation, no one was better qualified to develop and promote the Skyline route.

While Kirk Cecil and Lige Coalman were blazing the trail around Mount Jefferson during the summer of 1919, Cleator was already promoting the idea for a scenic highway along the Cascades. In an article for *Motor Land Magazine*, Cleator described a "grand scenic route," following a path previously available only to those able to manage the trail by foot or horseback.[183] Cleator aimed to open the High Cascades to the average person who could enjoy its natural wonders from the comfort of their car. With that goal in mind, he set out to survey and map the proposed route during the summer of 1920.

Cleator planned to begin the survey in mid-July after the higher-elevation snow had melted. His team would scout and map a route from Crater Lake north to Minto Pass, ending near Three Fingered Jack, where Cecil and Coalman had completed their work the previous summer. The task included scouting potential locations for shelters, campgrounds and recreational resorts along the route.

In addition to laying out the highway route, Cleator was also looking for spots to build several dozen shelters along the trail at roughly ten-mile intervals. The Skyline route was meant to intersect with existing Forest Service roads, providing access to proposed recreational sites at several high alpine lakes, including Marion, Pamelia, Fish, Big, Gold and Linton Lakes.[184]

When the Skyline party departed Crater Lake, the team included a Forest Service engineer, two grazing examiners, a cook and a packer to manage the horses.[185] Given the breadth and complexity of their duties, the expedition had a sizeable packing list. They carried surveying equipment, including an aneroid barometer for measuring atmospheric pressure. The aneroid was a smaller, nonliquid barometer better suited for determining elevation in the backcountry. Cleator also carried a compass and an Abney level for measuring slope angle. However, he didn't bring a measuring wheel, a common surveying instrument of the day. Instead, he paced off the trail distances by foot.[186]

In addition to their camp gear, food and surveying tools, Cleator brought his photography equipment. During the journey, he took hundreds of pictures highlighting the scenery and some of the engineering challenges along the proposed route. The team received additional shipments at various points on the trail, including hundreds of signs to mark their path. One of the shipments included several carrier pigeons, which the team used to communicate with Forest Service headquarters and coordinate their resupply from remote locations along the trail.[187]

The Forest Service borrowed the idea for pigeons from the U.S. Navy and started an experimental program in the Deschutes National Forest in 1919.[188] It was led by forest examiner William "Pigeon Bill" Sproat, a recent graduate of Yale's School of Forestry who was assigned to the Deschutes National Forest office in Bend. Sproat raised the pigeons with his wife and used them to send messages home while he was out in the field.

The pigeons were trained to carry notes in aluminum tubes attached to their legs and return to their cote at ranger stations located at Crater Lake, Klamath Lake, Prineville, Burns and Portland. The Forest Service also used the birds on mountaintop fire lookouts and sent them with truck crews fighting fires at remote locations. The pigeons could reportedly fly six hundred miles a day and up to seventy-five miles an hour, making them ideal for alerting the Forest Service about fast-moving fires along the Cascades. However, the program lasted only a few years—the pigeons were soon replaced by wireless radio sets, which were more effective and reliable.

## DESIGNING THE SKYLINE

Cleator kept a detailed diary of his daily activities during his four months on the trail. Many entries concerned mundane matters of logistics and weather. But his writings also revealed the trail's hardships and Cleator's vision for the scenic road. Historian Stuart Barker observed how Cleator's work on the Skyline Trail was deeply influenced by the ideas of the renowned landscape architect Frank Waugh, author of several well-known books on landscape design.[189]

Waugh was considered a pioneer in landscape design for recreational areas and known for his naturalistic style. He believed that man-made structures in nature should be made as inconspicuous as possible through simple design and the use of native materials. His ideas became a template for how the Forest Service and National Parks Service approached the design of early recreational facilities, trails and campgrounds during the 1920s.

Waugh visited Oregon during his five-month tour in 1917, examining recreational development in the national forests. During the trip, he made stops at Mount Hood, the Columbia River Gorge, and Oregon Caves. He returned to Oregon over the summer of 1920 to help the Forest Service develop its recreational plan for Mount Hood.[190] Waugh was closely involved in the design of the Mount Hood Loop Road. The project reflected many of his ideas about sequence, directional change and the use of scenic vistas for dramatic effect.[191]

Cleator was a student of Waugh's work, and the two men exchanged correspondence about the Skyline project. Cleator integrated many of Waugh's ideas into his route selection for the Skyline Road. Waugh's design philosophy emphasized the importance of scenic vistas when developing natural areas for public enjoyment.[192] He called these spots "paragraphic points," whose value could be maximized through deliberate trail design to present the landscape as a series of unfolding scenes.

Waugh believed that good trail design made maximum use of prominent natural features such as hills, mountains and lakes. That philosophy influenced Cleator's decision-making as he laid out the Skyline Trail. He carefully considered the sequence of scenic viewpoints when selecting his route and locating campsites. Cleator built the path around these paragraphic points, taking great care to avoid long segments of dull terrain lacking views and spectacular scenery.

Cleator understood that recreational trail design had different imperatives than trails created for other purposes such as administration, resource extraction and fire control. In keeping with Waugh's approach, he wanted to present the proposed Skyline Road as a curated journey showcasing the highlights of the Cascades. Cleator wrote to Waugh that he tried to pick a route highlighting "the ruggedness of the mountains, the alpine meadows, the high mesas and volcanic formations as intimately as possible."[193]

## THE SKYLINE SURVEY BEGINS

Cleator arrived in Medford on July 9, 1920, planning to purchase supplies and finalize logistics for the trip. Two days later, he left for Crater Lake, stopping at Union Creek, where the Forest Service was developing a recreational area. The site had a long history as a stopover along the Jacksonville to Fort Klamath Military Wagon Road, dating back to the 1860s.

By the late nineteenth century, Union Creek was a popular site for visitors traveling from the Rogue Valley for camping and fishing. Shortly after the turn of the century, the road was improved for auto traffic and became a popular rest stop for tourists on their way to Crater Lake. During the early 1920s, the Forest Service built a campground and ranger station and permitted the development of tourist cabins and a resort.

Cleator had been involved with planning the facilities at Union Creek and was curious to see the progress. Earlier that year, he had helped develop the comprehensive recreation plan for the location, which included summer home tracts, campgrounds and a resort site. Cleator personally did the landscape design plan for the site.[194] But when they stopped at Union Creek on their way to Crater Lake, Cleator was disappointed. He wrote in his diary that he was "not very favorable" about the project thus far.[195]

That evening, the party continued to Hamaker Meadows, where they camped along the Upper Rogue River. Upon their arrival at camp, Cleator realized that his luggage containing all his clothes and surveying instruments had been left in Medford. The next day, he arranged to have the lost baggage forwarded to the post office at Crater Lake while they continued to Diamond Lake, where they planned to make an extended camp.

During the stay at Diamond Lake, Cleator took extra time to circle the shoreline, taking pictures and studying the area for its recreation potential. He considered Diamond Lake one of the jewels of the Cascades and an excellent site for recreation. Cleator later argued against a proposal to dam

The Skyline survey pack train crossing the Spring River in the Umpqua National Forest at the beginning of the journey, late July 1920. *U.S. Forest Service.*

the lake for water storage. In 1922, he led the recreational survey to develop a lodge and tourist facilities at the lake.[196]

The weather at the lake was rainy and cold, but Cleator still managed to climb Mount Bailey, rising high above the lake, to gain a better view of his route north. The following day, the cook awoke suffering from a bad tooth in his upper jaw. Cleator made a note in his diary that the man was already missing all the teeth in his lower jaw. One of the grazing examiners offered to remove the offending tooth with a pair of automobile pliers. After laying the cook on the ground, the grazing examiner leveraged his knee against the man's chest and gave the tooth a firm yank with the pliers, apparently resolving the issue.[197]

Cleator left on horseback for Crater Lake the day after the successful dental procedure. After retrieving his lost luggage, he toured parts of the Rim Road, marveling at the "very excellent example of landscape engineering." Unfortunately, the expected shipment of Skyline Trail signs hadn't arrived with Cleator's luggage, so the party was forced to improvise a plan for marking the trail. They carved a series of vertical "skyline blazes" with a horizontal notch into trees along the route for the first forty

Frederick Cleator posting a Skyline sign, likely near the intersection of the Skyline and Minto Trails, October 1920. *U.S. Forest Service.*

miles.[198] It wasn't until later in August that they finally received the first shipment of metal signs.

In mid-July, Cleator again climbed Mount Bailey for another overview of his planned route north to the Three Sisters. A few days later, they began the first leg of the survey between Diamond Lake and the Kelsay Valley. Along the way, Cleator made careful notes about grade and elevation, clearly focused on the route's suitability for automobiles. He also made detailed notes about the topography, flora and soil quality.

During the first month of the survey, the team gradually adjusted to life on the trail. They had to overcome logistical challenges and missing horses. The team blazed difficult trail sections through rough, unmarked terrain while battling swarms of mosquitoes, especially around Waldo Lake. At one point, Cleator complained that he and the grazing examiner were having trouble with their socks. One had a pair that was too thin and the other a pair that was too thick. Eventually, they decided to swap socks, which provided immediate relief and "made us both feel like new men," according to Cleator's diary entry.[199]

Later in July, they began surveying the segment between Diamond Lake and Cowhorn Mountain. The two grazing examiners left for Bend on the twenty-fourth. One returned a few days later with four carrier pigeons for communication.[200] On the same day, Cleator climbed Cowhorn Mountain for a better view of the next section of their route. Cleator noted that the Forest Service didn't have accurate maps north of Cowhorn Mountain. Therefore, occasional peak-climbing was needed so a suitable route could be "grubbed out."[201]

From the top of Cowhorn, looking to the north, Cleator could see far across the Central Cascades to Mount Hood in the distance. He took panoramic photographs and collected medicinal flowers for the grazing examiner/camp dentist who failed to make the summit. Cleator had left him earlier, "sick under a tree below with bowel trouble."

At the end of July, they moved their camp to Crescent Lake, picking a spot with spectacular views of Diamond Peak. In his notes, Cleator gushed that "the Skyline is going to be a great recreation trail. The road may be some time building, but from Crater Lake Park to Crescent Lake, at least it is as simple and as cheap road building as I ever saw in a timbered country."[202] He considered Crescent Lake a good site for developing campgrounds and summer homes since the lake already had a "passable auto road" connecting it to Bend. Cleator surveyed around the entire lake before deciding to route the road along the eastern shore.[203]

Skyline survey members on the east end of Crescent Lake before leaving camp, early August 1920. *U.S. Forest Service.*

On August 1, Cleator gave his crew a rest day while he summited Diamond Peak to take photographs. That day, he wrote, "I am beginning to think that a Skyline Trail the full length of the Cascades in Washington and Oregon, joining a similar trail in the Sierras of California, would be a great tourist advertisement. For that matter, it might be continued thru [*sic*] British Columbia and up the Alaska highlands. This is a future work, but it would be fine to plan upon."[204]

For several reasons, his inspiration from the top of Diamond Peak about a long-distance trail stretching from Canada to California is significant. Cleator was likely the first person to articulate a concept for what eventually became the Pacific Crest Trail. At the same time, it was a hint that Cleator may have doubted the feasibility of building a scenic highway along the route, perhaps realizing that a walking trail was a better alternative.

During the trip, Cleator was intent on improving his picture-taking techniques. In early August, he met a photographer from Eugene along the trail between Crescent and Crater Lakes. The man was traveling with a portable darkroom and offered to develop some of Cleator's photos to assess their quality. After examining the pictures, they spent an entire evening discussing photography and tips for improving Cleator's pictures.

On August 7, the party moved north to Odell Lake, which Cleator observed "many consider the most beautiful water surface in Oregon."[205]

A member of the Skyline survey helping Frederick Cleator take a panorama picture from the top of South Sister, early September 1920. *U.S. Forest Service.*

Members of the Skyline survey transferring supplies from a hayrack to boats on Odell Lake, August 1920. *U.S. Forest Service.*

They made camp at Trapper Creek on the northwest shore. Since the party had been eating fish for several weeks, they were excited to purchase a sheep for a change of cuisine. The next day, Cleator set out for Waldo Lake but missed his destination. He later noted that the section of the trail between Odell and Waldo Lakes was in poor condition and needed improvement.

They finally reached Waldo Lake the following day. Cleator took elevation measurements along the route with his aneroid barometer. At one trail intersection, they found "caustic remarks" written on a trail sign, asking, "Why don't the Forest Service clean up its trails?" In his notes, Cleator conceded that the "Forest Service has been somewhat remiss" in maintaining the overgrown section of trail between Odell and Waldo Lakes.[206]

On August 10, Cleator climbed to the top of Maiden Peak, a steep-sided shield volcano and the highest point between Diamond Peak and Mount Bachelor. From there, Cleator planned their advance to the north, adjusting his route to hit scenic vistas and avoid overly steep grades. Cleator remained in camp the next day to catch up on paperwork, organize his photographs, and catalogue plant specimens.

On August 13, sixty Skyline Trail signs that were missing from their initial supplies were delivered to camp. The next day, the party moved on to Waldo Lake. On the fifteenth, Cleator climbed the ridgeline of Mount Ray at the southern end of Waldo Lake. From there, he was able to pick a good route between Waldo Lake and Twins Peak to the east. Cleator wrote in his diary that Waldo Lake had been the most interesting spot of the trip thus far, calling it "one of the most valuable scenic assets of the Skyline."[207] He added that there was "no lake that has greater recreation possibilities" but noted that plentiful mosquitoes detracted from its wonders.

A few days later, the party moved camp to Irish and Taylor Lakes, about halfway between Waldo and Cultus Lakes. Cleator reported that one of the horses had been missing since leaving Waldo Lake. Cleator climbed Taylor Butte from the new camp to get an overview of the next section of trail stretching north to the Three Sisters.

Toward the end of August, Cleator took a five-day break from the trail for a stopover in Bend. While there, he arranged for resupply, caught up on paperwork and developed his photographs from the first part of the trip. He also met with the Deschutes National Forest supervisor to discuss the Skyline Road project.

While in Bend, Cleator stocked up on reading material for his remaining time on the trail. He bought two novels and a short story collection, all by the famous American adventure writer James Oliver Curwood. It's appropriate

Skyline survey members on the shore of Elk Lake with South Sister and Broken Top in the background, late August 1920. *U.S. Forest Service.*

that Cleator was a fan of Curwood. They were both from the Midwest and around the same age. Curwood had dropped out of the University of Michigan to pursue journalism, while Cleator had dropped out of the University of Minnesota for forestry work. Both men had worked in Alaska around the same time and were inspired by its landscape.

For Curwood, his time in Alaska was the beginning of a successful writing career. By the early 1920s, he was one of the best-selling authors in the United States, writing adventure novels set in the wilds of the Northwest in the vein of Jack London and Zane Grey. Sadly, Curwood died at a young age in the late 1920s from an infection that began while on a fishing trip. But before his death, he became an ardent conservationist and worked passionately on behalf of environmental causes in his home state of Michigan.[208]

While in Bend, Cleator picked up a copy of Curwood's *River's End*, his most successful novel, and *The Valley of Silent Men*. Both were romantic adventures set in the Canadian Northwest. But Cleator's taste in reading material was practical as well as literary. In his diary, Cleator mentions buying a copy of *Good Housekeeping* magazine to bring back to camp.

On August 26, Cleator rejoined the survey party as they made their next camp at Elk Lake. While in Bend, Cleator discussed the best route around the Three Sisters with Deschutes National Forest officials. He was inclined toward the western side of the crest, following the existing trail between Elk Lake and the McKenzie Highway. However, he also saw the appeal of creating a high route along the eastern side of the Three Sisters and believed that one should eventually be developed.

While at Elk Lake, Cleator wrote that "the trail is now the main objective, however, and as far as the road is concerned, snow studies along the Skyline trail should be made before the road is started."[209] The observation again reveals Cleator's concerns about the practicality of maintaining an automobile road at such elevations. Even as he laid out the route for the proposed road, Cleator seemed to harbor doubts that it would ever be built.

The survey party spent the last week of August scouting the area west of Elk Lake, with side trips to Elk Mountain, Sparks Lake, Sisters Mirror Lake, Red Butte and Horse Lake. On August 30, the cook narrowly escaped serious injury when a fire broke out in camp. The blaze destroyed Cleator's tent, bedding and clothes. Fortunately, he was able to save his diary, camera and film. After the fire, Cleator departed for a three-day excursion to the Green Lakes, exploring the high plateau between Broken Top and South Sister.

On the last day of August, Cleator climbed the west pinnacle of Broken Top to survey a possible route along the eastern side of The Sisters. The next day, he scaled South Sister via the eastern ridgeline from Green Lakes, likely using the same route that Judge Waldo took in September 1883. At the top, Cleator took notes and photographs on his planned route west of the Three Sisters.

Before descending, Cleator released one of the carrier pigeons with an undisclosed message.[210] That night, they returned to camp later than expected, tired and hungry from two days of challenging climbs. Before falling asleep, Cleator wrote in his diary, "The camp at Green Lakes has been, taking everything into consideration, the most interesting camp we have had."

The next day, they left Green Lakes and moved to the next campsite at Separation Creek, set in the draw below Chambers Lakes between South and Middle Sisters. Cleator scouted a trail from Green Lakes down to Sparks Lake, following Fall Creek on his way down. At the bottom, he searched for the Indigenous pictographs near Devils Lake and recorded some questionable mythology about their origin in his diary.

While passing by Devil's Lake, Cleator scouted a beautiful spot for a campground that he thought would be a popular stop for tourists along the Skyline route. After leaving Devil's Lake, he investigated a potential site for

*Right*: An unnamed member of the Skyline survey holding a carrier pigeon used for sending messages back to Forest Service headquarters, August 1920. *Forest History Society*.

*Below*: A Skyline survey member releasing a carrier pigeon from the top of South Sister, early September 1920. *U.S. Forest Service*.

*Opposite*: A Curtiss "Jenny" single-engine biplane flying an aerial fire patrol over Mount Jefferson, circa 1920. Cleator was tasked with locating potential airfields as part of the Skyline survey. *Oregon State University*.

a backcountry airstrip on Wickiup Plain and another site near their camp at Separation Creek. One of Cleator's tasks that summer was to scout airfield sites for the Forest Service's Aerial Forest-Fire Patrol Program, which had begun the previous summer.

In 1919, the U.S. Army Air Service began flying fire-spotting patrols over California and Oregon with Forest Service observers. The program was led by Colonel Henry "Hap" Arnold, commander of Crissy Field in San Francisco and the Army Air Service in California. Arnold was looking for a way to maintain funding for military aviation after the end of World War I. He believed that helping the Forest Service fight fires was one way to do it.[211]

That summer, Arnold's pilots began flying fire-spotting patrols out of airfields in Salem and Roseburg. By the end of the season, additional patrols were flying from Portland, Eugene and Medford.[212] Unfortunately, accidents and communication challenges plagued the program. By the mid-1920s, the Forest Service decided that using mountaintop spotters for fire detection was a better option, and the aviation program withered.

During the first week of September, Cleator's survey party blazed a trail along the western side of the Three Sisters between Rock Mesa and Obsidian Cliffs. In his diary, Cleator said that they followed "an old Indian trail now unused almost except by a few transient sheepmen," and insisted that the trail had not been blazed.[213] From his comment, it's unclear how much Cleator knew about the trail's history. While it may not have been formally "blazed," it had been used for hundreds of years by Oregon's Indigenous people, followed by Judge Waldo, Cy Bingham, Dee Wright, the Mazamas and others.

In Cleator's defense, his task on the route was far more difficult than those who went before him. Scouting a scenic highway through the mountains was much more technically challenging than following a footpath. Cleator went to great pains to find a route of less than 5 percent grade that avoided complex engineering challenges while still offering scenic value. Due to the rough topography and his desire to maximize views, Cleator needed to keep the trail at around 6,700 feet on that section of the route. But he also had to contend with the challenge of late-season snowpack at higher elevations.

On September 7, the party moved to their next camp at White Branch Creek near Obsidian Cliffs. From there, they spent the next ten days scouting a route through the rugged terrain between Obsidian Cliffs and McKenzie Highway. By the early 1920s, the area around McKenzie Pass was already popular with campers and tourists. That summer, work crews were busy making improvements along the road over the summit.

The day after making their new camp, Cleator went exploring and climbed a horseshoe-shaped cinder cone on the flanks of North Sister. From there, he took notes and photographs of their next major challenge: finding a route through the rugged lava fields surrounding Belknap Crater. Cleator named his viewpoint "Cinderella," seeming pleased with the clever wordplay on the Three Sisters theme while alluding to its volcanic origin.

The name appeared on the Skyline Trail map published the following year, but it didn't stick. Subsequent maps instead referred to Cleator's "Cinderella" as Collier Cone, named for George Collier, a professor of chemistry and physics at the University of Oregon who explored the region in the 1880s.[214] Cleator had better luck naming other landmarks. For example, Betty Lake, a small body of water near Waldo Lake, is named after his daughter.

Cleator was particularly taken by the scenery around McKenzie Pass but understood that road construction through that section would be challenging. On September 11, Cleator wrote, "We should have a month to figure the best route between the McKenzie and Santiam roads but will do our best in the time we have. The lava flows north of here are a corker on the shoes and nerves."[215]

One point of uncertainty was how to proceed through the lava fields surrounding Belknap Crater and onward to Mount Washington. Cleator believed there might be an option for going to the east of Mount Washington, skirting around Black Crater, but he was concerned that the route would entail a significant loss of elevation. Cleator seemed to prefer a path along the eastern side of Belknap Crater, then circling to the west around Mount

Washington. He acknowledged that this route would entail a considerable feat of engineering but felt that going through the lava fields would "add immensely to the interest of the Skyline Trail."[216]

They spent several days in camp during mid-September due to the weather. Cleator took the time to catch up on his notes. During breaks in the weather, they occasionally ventured out to blaze trails and post signs along the path. Meanwhile, two of his men traveled to McKenzie Bridge to pick up supplies. On September 15, Cleator rode over to Linton Lake. The next day he climbed Scott Mountain, envisioning the summit as an attractive side trip off the Skyline route.

On September 17, the party moved their camp to a meadow near Pole Bridge, along the McKenzie Highway between Hand and Scott Lakes.[217] The next day, Cleator climbed a pair of red cinder cones east of Scott Mountain and dubbed them "Twin Craters." Two days later, he summited Belknap Crater, the dominating shield volcano north of McKenzie Pass. From that viewpoint, Cleator determined that "the proper place for the Skyline trail is over the beautiful mesas east of Belknap Crater," offering views of eastern Oregon.[218] However, that was not the route that eventually appeared on the Skyline Trail map published the following year.

Instead, Cleator's revised route crossed the McKenzie Highway near Hand and Scott Lakes before cutting through the lava fields west of Belknap Crater and Mount Washington, then onward to Big Lake. Cleator's notes in the final trip report explained his reasoning for the change. He called the section of trail between the McKenzie Highway and Santiam Road the "most difficult along the entire route."[219] The decision for the more direct route to the west of Belknap Crater was simply a matter of cost.

After descending Belknap Crater on the 19th, Cleator discovered that his horse was missing from where he left it at the base of the cone. With no alternative, Cleator loaded his saddle and gear on his back, including all his photography equipment. After struggling several miles through the lava fields back to McKenzie Highway, Cleator dropped everything except for the horse's bridle and his jacket, camera and film. Then he walked several miles down the road, only to find his horse waiting for him just outside the camp.

The next morning began a stretch of unfavorable weather, limiting their ability to work. Cleator reported rain and snow lasting several days that flooded their camp and soaked all the bedding. By that point in the journey, trail fatigue was setting in. On September 24, Cleator fired the cook, noting in his diary that his service was "not very satisfactory."[220]

After dismissing the cook, the remaining team members left for Sisters through heavy rain and snow. They spent the next few days inspecting the area around Black Butte, Suttle Lake and Camp Sherman. Cleator was interested in seeing the progress of the recreational cabins along the Metolius River. The areas opposite Camp Sherman had been among the Forest Service's first recreational residence tracts in Oregon, starting in 1916.[221] Cleator had personally surveyed many of these sites and was curious to check on their progress.

On September 27, the crew left Sisters and made their next camp at Four-Mile Spring along the McKenzie Highway. This spot was intended to be the last permanent camp of the survey. From there, they could make shorter excursions to the endpoint near Minto Pass, roughly where Kirk Cecil and Lige Coalman had ended their survey around Mount Jefferson the previous summer. Cleator hiked to the top of Black Crater the next day to study the terrain. He mentioned several times in his diary that he wanted to push the Skyline route east to include Black Crater; however, that detour never made it into the final plan.

Early October brought more frustrations with inclement weather and missing horses. On October 4, they broke camp at Four-Mile Spring and

The Skyline camp at Four Mile Springs off McKenzie Highway near the end of the survey, late September 1920. *U.S. Forest Service.*

sent some of their equipment down to Sisters as the survey neared its end. Cleator sent two men south to post trail signs while he went north to scout the section of trail between the Santiam Road and Minto Pass.

On October 7, Cleator moved to a final camp at Big Lake, which he considered one of the most beautiful spots of the trip. However, he believed that it deserved a better name. In his diary, Cleator proposed calling it "Martha Lake," given its proximity to Mount Washington, but the name never took hold.

Cleator spent his last few days finalizing and photographing the route. On October 9, they packed up camp in the rain and began the long ride back to Sisters. Cleator seemed eager to return to civilization but also nostalgic about the summer's journey. In Sisters, he helped clean gear, pay bills and load equipment. Later in the day, he got a ride to Redmond, then caught a night train to Portland, arriving home early the following morning. The entire journey from Crater Lake to Minto Pass had taken precisely four months.

## The Final Report and Map

After Cleator returned to Portland, he began working on his final report. Meanwhile, the Forest Service was preparing a detailed map of the Skyline route that would be published the following year. Cleator's final report covered his entire reconnaissance from Crater Lake to Minto Pass, just a few miles north of Three Fingered Jack.

According to his final calculations, the route's average elevation was 5,300 feet, reaching as high as 6,500 feet in some spots. Based on the average seasonal snowpack, Cleator estimated that the proposed road could be used only around three months of the year. He speculated that it would be used chiefly for tourist travel but also saw a role for fire protection, logistics and grazing.[222]

Cleator offered several options for altering the mapped route in his final report. The first involved using the newly constructed road segment between Elk Lake and Crane Prairie, part of Century Drive, rather than the more direct route from Taylor Lake along the crest to South Sister. The second option involved the eastern route around the Three Sisters from Sparks Lake and rejoining the ridgeline near Big Lake. While Cleator seemed to prefer this route, he conceded that building it would be challenging and expensive.[223]

Cleator's final cost estimate for the project assumed a roadway of ten to sixteen feet wide, made of earth. He believed that most of the road could be completed at a grade of 5 percent, with only a few short sections of at most 6 percent. Although Cleator expressed confidence about the project in his official communication, he must have understood that the proposal would entail an enormous feat of engineering. His final cost estimate for the road project was around $1.5 million—an astronomical amount for a Forest Service roadbuilding project during that time.[224]

The following year, Cleator's work on the Skyline route gained widespread attention as boosters aggressively promoted the idea as part of a campaign to increase tourism. In 1920, the Oregon legislature created a Tourist and Information Bureau, financed by the state, with board members appointed by the governor. Although the board lasted only a few years, it actively promoted Oregon as an outdoor recreation paradise, hoping to spur the state's fledgling tourism industry.

In 1921, the Tourist and Information Bureau paid to develop and print a recreational map based on Cleator's survey. The Forest Service tasked a draftsman named Theodore Flynn to compile the map based on Cleator's notes.[225] Although Flynn had only begun his cartographic career a few years earlier, he produced a remarkably vivid and detailed three-piece strip map depicting Cleator's route. It was a notable achievement at a time when only around 20 percent of the national forests were accurately mapped.

Flynn's trail map covered the entire route from Mount Hood to Crater Lake. It depicted national forest boundaries, roads, campgrounds, scenic viewpoints, ranger stations and even the locations of Forest Service telephone lines in case of emergencies. It showed a variety of services and supply points along the route, including stores, post offices, lodgings and gas stations. It also had locations of feed and water for saddle and pack animals. The bottom of the page had a matrix showing the mileage between campsites along the route.[226]

The map had over thirty suggested camps, including many of the same spots used by Cleator's survey. The final route hewed very closely to the path blazed by Kirk Cecil and Lige Coalman in 1919 and Cleator's party in 1920. However, the northernmost section between Clackamas Lake and Government Camp was not depicted as a trail but followed the existing Forest Service road passing by Clear Lake, Frog Lake and Summit Butte.

The free pamphlet was geared toward nonmotorized travel and served as a marketing device for the proposed Skyline Road. The booklet was an unabashed piece of promotional literature, selling Oregon as "the land where dreams come true" set in "the greatest panorama of outdoor attractions in all America." The route was billed as "a walking trip through one of the most scenic sections of the United States," passing through five national forests.[227]

The route's final advertised length from Mount Hood to Crater Lake was 260 miles, with an average elevation of 5,400 feet. Due to the seasonal snowpack, recreational travel was recommended only from July through the end of September. According to the pamphlet, the route was marked by over five hundred metal signs reading "Oregon Skyline" set at quarter and half-mile intervals. These were later supplemented by swaths of white fabric to increase their visibility through the thick forest.

The pamphlet advised that those traveling by foot needed at least one month to complete the journey but suggested that two months would offer a more enjoyable experience. However, a pack trip by horse was recommended for "best satisfaction." While the trail was not yet accessible for automobiles, the pamphlet promised that a planned road along the route would soon "open these almost unknown scenic attractions to tourist travel and human enjoyment."

The reverse side of the map was filled with practical advice for those attempting the route, including tips on fire prevention, sanitation, trail etiquette and regulations on hunting and fishing. The text also offered notes of caution, discouraging visitors from embarking on the journey unprepared. Travelers were warned that the trip involved "rough mountain travel… under conditions of physical hardship."

Some segments of the trail were appropriately described as "dim and hard to follow." A disclaimer noted that routes branching off the main Skyline Trail "cannot be warranted in any way." At that time, the only resupply points between Crater Lake and Mount Hood were at Odell and Crescent Lakes. Therefore, travelers were advised to make prior arrangements to receive deliveries along the route. The summer after Cleator's survey, the Forest Service reported that it was already receiving inquiries about recreational travel along Skyline Trail by horseback and foot. One party reportedly asked about following the range north through Washington to the Canadian border.[228]

# THE FOREST SERVICE'S FIRST LONG-DISTANCE RECREATIONAL TRAIL

The Skyline survey and trail work of 1919–20 was a remarkable accomplishment, particularly given the relatively small investment of resources. Over two summers, a few foresters had blazed and mapped one of the longest contiguous recreational trails in the United States. In many respects, it was an achievement far ahead of its time. It was the Forest Service's first long-distance recreational trail and one of the few such routes in the country.

One year to the day after Cleator finished his Skyline survey, Benton MacKaye published the first article introducing the idea for the Appalachian Trail. MacKaye's proposal, appearing in the *Journal of the American Institute of Architects*, earned him the title of "Father of the AT."[229] But at the time, the trail was little more than a loosely linked network of regional footpaths supported by community hiking clubs across New England and New York.

The Skyline Trail had been fully surveyed and mapped while the Appalachian Trail was still on the drawing board. The next step was transforming it into a scenic highway. Cleator would be closely involved in that quixotic effort, even as he took on other responsibilities for planning and developing recreational infrastructure across Oregon and Washington.

Over the next two decades, the trail would evolve in fits and starts, but not into the form originally intended. Cleator's work over the summer of 1920 had a meaningful and lasting impact, but ultimately the road was never built. Instead, the trail developed into something very different from what the Forest Service had envisioned. That result reflected changing values about outdoor recreation and a growing desire to preserve and protect the invaluable wilderness landscapes along the Skyline Trail.

# 5

# SELLING THE SKYLINE

## *Outdoor Recreation in the Age of Auto Tourism*

Even before Cleator began the Skyline survey, the Forest Service and influential boosters were busy promoting the idea of a scenic highway along the Cascade Crest. The success of the Columbia River Highway and plans for the Mount Hood Loop Road generated enthusiasm for a similar scenic route along the Cascades. Road supporters included prominent Oregonians like Lewis McArthur and Fred Kiser. It also had strong backing from the Oregon State Chamber of Commerce, the Tourist and Information Bureau and the Oregon State Motor Association.[230]

The Forest Service's official statements suggested that the agency strongly supported the road concept. Historian William Tweed suggested that their enthusiasm may have been partly rooted in bureaucratic competition with the recently established National Park Service.[231] Stuart Barker also found evidence for this theory in the correspondence between Frederick Cleator, Frank Waugh and Forest Service leaders. Their contemporaneous notes suggested that the Skyline Road could be a way of solidifying Forest Service control over the Cascades and forestalling the creation of other national parks in the state.[232]

In the decades after the establishment of Crater Lake National Park, there were several campaigns aimed at creating another national park around Mount Hood, potentially removing the area from the National Forest System.[233] After his 1919 trip, Fred Kiser had argued for turning the entire Cascade Range into a national park.[234] Julius Stone, a midwestern businessman who accompanied Kiser on the trip, was another vocal advocate for creating a Cascades national park that would include the entire backbone of the range above five thousand feet.[235]

Beyond bureaucratic rivalry, the Forest Service touted other potential benefits of the Skyline Road concept. Chief among them was the potential economic value derived from improving access to timber, grazing areas and other natural resources. The Forest Service argued that Skyline Road would link six existing trans-Cascade routes, opening new routes for commercial traffic over the mountains. Fire protection was another important argument. The Forest Service claimed that the Skyline Road could support mountain airbases for aerial fire patrols.

But the main argument for the road was about expanding opportunities for recreation and tourism and the promise of turning the Cascades into "a tremendous playground for all Americans."[236] The road would enable new recreational development, including summer homes, hotels, service stations and stores. Road boosters promised it would become "one of the greatest scenic drives of America."[237]

Many of Oregon's leading newspapers jumped on the Skyline Road bandwagon. Just weeks after Cleator's survey, the *Oregon Sunday Journal* published a lengthy article portraying the project in the most favorable light.[238] Based on the results of Cleator's survey, the road was deemed "entirely feasible," according to reports. Several news articles pointed out that the revised cost had come in lower than the original estimate of $2.5 million. However, the more favorable number was based on a barebones estimate for building a narrow, ten-foot road. Even at the low estimate, the Skyline route would be exorbitantly expensive compared with other forest roads.

Undeterred by the costs, road promoters suggested that tourism revenues could be used to finance a later expansion. At the time, few observers questioned the rosy assumptions about the road's potential to draw tourists. The *Oregon Sunday Journal* quoted a Forest Service official predicting that "no state in the Union will have a more popular highway."

Bold claims about the Skyline Road were based on comparisons to other scenic routes, such as the Columbia River Highway. A front-page feature in *The Oregonian* proclaimed, "What the Columbia highway is to the great river gorge, the Skyline will become to the Cascade Range."[239] One report predicted that once opened, the Skyline Road would be "thronged by cars bearing license tags from every state of the union."[240]

Great enthusiasm for ambitious roadbuilding projects was typical at the time. Oregon's automobile associations, commercial clubs and civic organizations were strong supporters of the Good Roads Movement, which focused on improving rural byways.[241] Between 1910 and 1920, Oregon went from having only a few miles of improved roads outside urban areas to over seven hundred miles of paved roads.[242] In 1919, Oregon became the first state in the nation to establish a gasoline tax to help finance road development projects. For supporters of the Good Road Movement, roadbuilding, recreation and economic development were inextricably linked.

Many of Oregon's most scenic stretches of highway were built during this era of frenetic roadbuilding. Work on the Columbia River Highway began in 1913 and was completed by 1922. Construction of the Crater Lake Rim Road started the same year under the supervision of the Army Corps of Engineers. In 1914, work began on the Oregon Coast Highway from Astoria to California and continued into the 1930s. From 1920 to 1924, the Forest Service worked with state officials to develop the Mount Hood Loop Road as part of the agency's recreation plan.

In Central Oregon, construction began on Century Drive during the early 1920s. The route started just outside Bend and offered the first reliable access to the higher-elevation recreational areas of the Deschutes National Forest. The road passed by Bachelor Butte and through the high

An automobile driving along the McKenzie Highway near Frog Camp with the Three Sisters in the background, circa 1930. *U.S. Forest Service.*

lakes region before connecting to the Dalles-California Highway. The return trip to Bend made a loop of roughly one hundred miles, giving the route its name. The section of Century Drive between Elk and Lava Lakes was considered part of the proposed Skyline Road route.

Rising levels of automobile ownership and aggressive roadbuilding programs became catalysts for a boom in outdoor recreation during the 1920s.[243] The *Oregon Sunday Journal* heralded the transition from "hay burners" (horses) to the new age of auto-based tourism. The paper suggested that automobiles would offer access to remote parts of the Cascades rarely visited by tourists, making them "the common property of the motoring public of Oregon."[244] Meanwhile, *The Oregonian* predicted that the Skyline Road would generate great appeal for tourists in the age of the automobile, in which "the habit of making long trips by foot or horseback has long since disappeared."[245]

In 1924, *The Oregonian* ran a series on the "Scenic Highways of the Future," starting with the Skyline Road. The paper enlisted the help of the well-known Portland pictorial artist Fred Routledge to illustrate an idealized map of the Skyline route.[246] Routledge was known for his bird's-eye picture maps. His work often featured man-made wonders set against a backdrop of Oregon's iconic landscapes. Some of his most recognizable images include illustrations of the Cascade Locks, Portland General Electric's hydroelectric plant at Willamette Falls and the Columbia River Highway.[247]

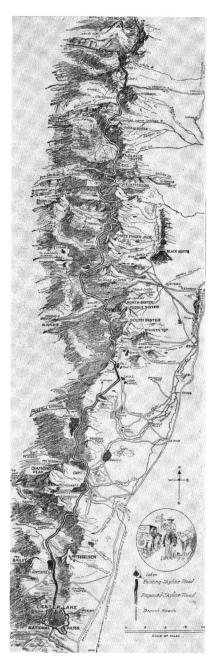

The proposed plan for the Skyline Road as depicted by noted illustrator Fred Routledge, 1924. *The Sunday Oregonian* and the *Oregon Historical Society*.

Later in his career, Routledge's work turned to automotive tourism and highways. He became known for creating distinctive tourist maps and guidebooks, work often associated with the Good Roads Movement. His book *Pictorial Oregon—The Wonderland* featured oversized maps of the state's scenic auto routes. In the 1924 article about the Skyline Road, *The Oregonian* claimed that Routledge's picture map showed "better than words" what might be accomplished by opening the Cascades to motorists. [248]

## Early Travelers on the Skyline

The Skyline Road concept had many vocal supporters. However, they generally represented a narrow interest group—specifically, tourism promotors and the automobile lobby. A less vocal but equally passionate group saw the value in leaving the trail as it was. This group worried that an auto route along the crest would destroy what made the Cascades a unique place to visit. Among the Skyline Road skeptics was the famous writer and critic Walter Prichard Eaton.

Eaton was a professor of playwriting at Yale and a prolific author. He was an Easterner by birth and education but often traveled to the West for wilderness adventures. In the summer of 1921, Eaton spent six weeks in the High Cascades, escorted by famed Oregon photographer Fred Kiser. Eaton and Kiser had become friends during a two-week trip to Glacier National Park in 1916. Afterward, Kiser invited Eaton to Oregon, promising to show him "some of the most wonderful scenery in the world."[249]

During Eaton's trip to Oregon, he and Kiser covered lengthy segments of the Skyline Trail between Crater Lake and Mount Hood. After returning home, Eaton wrote a glowing travelogue of his adventure for the *New York Times*. He declared the trail "undoubtedly one of the finest escapes from civilization conveniently available in the United States."[250] But he was less enthusiastic about the plan to turn the rugged backcountry route into a highway. Eaton worried that auto tourism would "breed hotels and tin cans" and preferred to "have the Cascades left just as they are, wild and hard."

Eaton argued adamantly to preserve the Skyline for nonmotorized travel, suggesting that "any real lover of the mountains prefers to view them from the saddle of a cayuse, not the seat of a Cadillac."[251] He advised his readers: "If you love the wilderness, go to the Cascades while the Skyline Trail is just that—a trail—a dim track for tough horses and hardy men and women—

and you'll have forever a wonderful memory of an America which is vanishing."

Eaton's trip on the Skyline inspired two books the following year. The first, *Skyline Camps*, was an extended version of his *New York Times* article, offering a literary travelogue of his wilderness journeys across New England, Montana and Oregon. In the book, Eaton declared that the Cascades, unlike any other range in America, had a "beauty and a haunting mystery all its own."[252] His rare moments of disappointment came during his times away from the trail, such as a visit to Bend, which he declared a "Little City That Takes Itself Seriously." He made special note of the town's "hideous" architecture.[253]

The noted author and critic Walter Prichard Eaton recounted his journey along the Skyline Trail in a 1922 travelog titled *Skyline Camps*. *Oregon Historical Society.*

The Skyline Trail also appeared in another of Eaton's books that year, part of his popular Boy Scout adventure series. Eaton set the fictionalized story at Crater Lake and managed to work his opinion about the road into the narrative. At the end of the journey, one of his characters comments on the looming threat to the Skyline, lamenting "that someday Oregon is going to build into a highway right up along the spine of the Cascades."[254]

Although Eaton and Kiser disagreed on the Skyline Road, they found common ground in their love of the Cascades. Kiser provided photographs and illustrations for both of Eaton's books. In the acknowledgement, Eaton praised Kiser's skill as a nature photographer and outdoorsman, thanking him for his companionship during their weeks together traveling along the Skyline route.

After Eaton's article and books were published, the *Oregon Daily Journal* noted the author's disapproval of the road project. The paper agreed that most of the road's supporters likely shared Eaton's concerns. It acknowledged that "behind the megaphone of the appeal for broadening of the Skyline trail is the small group who have traversed the dim track. They are the people who love the route because of its arduous character, its loneliness, its altitude, its unartificialized magnificence, and its glorious vistas."[255] Nevertheless, the paper ultimately defended the auto route, noting that the trail's difficulty excluded too many citizens from experiencing its wonders.

The *Journal* argued that for the benefit of the majority, "even the wilderness must be pierced with modernness."

Eaton's fame helped introduce the Skyline Trail to a national audience, but most people who traveled the trail during the 1920s did so in obscurity. One such early hiker was Peter Parsons, a Swedish immigrant who came to Oregon in 1909. Like many migrants of the era, Parsons was drawn to Oregon for economic reasons. He traveled to the United States by steamship with a friend from Germany named Otto Witt. But when the ship's captain allegedly got into an argument with Otto, the two friends jumped ship together in Portland. Parsons forfeited six month's wages when he decided to join his friend.[256] Days later, the two men were arrested for trespassing. Through their limited English, they begged the judge for clemency. Instead of jail, he sent them to work at a lumberyard in Mill City.[257]

Parsons lived in Mill City off and on for the next two decades, working just enough to support various adventures into the mountains. In 1915, he was among a group of men helping Lige Coalman and Dee Wright haul construction material to the top of Mount Hood to build the summit fire lookout. For a brief time, he served in the U.S. Army before returning to Oregon in the early 1920s.

In 1923, Parsons left Mill City on an epic hiking adventure, planning to cover nearly 1,800 miles from Oregon to Mexico. He set out on the Skyline Trail and continued into California, taking a route like that of modern-day hikers on the Pacific Crest Trail. Unfortunately, Parsons didn't quite make his goal of reaching Mexico and stopped short in the Mojave Desert.

Parsons's mode of travel was a stark contrast to that of travelers like Eaton and Kiser, who went with a large entourage of packers carrying food, camping supplies and photography equipment. In contrast, Parsons was remarkably self-sufficient, traveling by foot and carrying his gear. His kit included a basic tarp tent, pistol and rifle, axe, field glass, compass, frying pan, quilted sleeping bag, journal and pencil and a folding Kodak camera. He subsisted on a diet of rice, beans, flour, peanuts, raisins and bacon and hunted to supplement the dried food.

After hiking through California, Parsons returned to Mill City to work over the fall and winter. The following year, he attempted an even more audacious route, walking from the Mexican border north along the Rocky Mountains to Canada. From there, he continued to Mount Rainier, down the Cascades and back to Mill City on a remarkable adventure that took him four and a half months.

Early Skyline Trail hiker Peter Parsons, 1928. *Courtesy of Barney Scout Mann.*

Although Parsons didn't follow an established trail and occasionally took rides, trail historian Barney Scout Mann still credits him as the first person to complete something resembling today's Continental Divide Trail. Mann discovered the epic journey because of a note that Parsons left in the summit register on Mount Jefferson at the end of his trip. That led Mann to Parsons's journals and photos, verifying his enormous accomplishment. Sadly, Parsons died in 1930 under mysterious circumstances while attempting to hike and canoe to the Arctic Circle through Alberta, Canada.

Parsons's journey along the Skyline represented one extreme of the experience during the 1920s—an arduous and solitary adventure. The pack trips led by Portland attorney Eugene Dowling were on the other end of the spectrum. For several summers during the late 1920s, Dowling led organized rides along the trail that were open to outdoors novices.[258] Dowling was a friend of Frederick Cleator and an experienced outdoorsman who offered the trips as a nonprofit venture under the name Cascade Micque Tours. The cost for an eighteen-day Skyline adventure was one hundred dollars, which included food, horses, equipment and transportation to the starting point.

Dowling led his first trip in 1926 with a party of twenty.[259] The trips began at Olallie Meadow, south of Mount Hood, and generally followed the path

Members of a Dowling pack trip at the foot of Mount Jefferson, late 1920s. *Mazama Library and Historical Collection.*

Female members of a Dowling pack trip resting at a cabin near Waldo Lake, late 1920s. *Mazama Library and Historical Collection.*

of Cleator's 1920 Skyline route. However, instead of crossing the lava fields over McKenzie Pass, Dowling's trips detoured east for two days, passing by Suttle Lake with a stopover in Sisters. From there, they followed a similar path of today's Metolius-Windigo Trail, rejoining the Skyline route around Wickiup Plain. After stops at Elk Lake and Lava Lake, the tour rejoined Cleator's track near Irish Lake and followed the Skyline route for the remainder of the way to Crater Lake.

The trip covered fifteen to twenty miles per day and lasted eighteen days. After a break at Crater Lake, Dowling would lead a different group back along the same path. Although the tours involved hiking and riding between camps, pack animals carried the tents and equipment while hired cooks prepared meals. The trip's advertisement promised "gorgeous scenery, excellent food, good horses, good fishing" for those seeking a packaged adventure along the Skyline.

Although Dowling's tours received a glowing review in *The Oregonian*, interest in the trips faded after a few years. In 1929, he offered his last organized Skyline tour to a group of physicians visiting Portland for a medical conference.[260] Cleator later speculated that the trips, however spectacular, were too arduous for the average tourist.[261]

Dowling's organized tours reflected something about the changing character of the Skyline route. As the trail became more established, the trips were billed as less arduous and more accessible for average tourists. This shift was partly a matter of marketing by the trail's boosters. Oregon's tourism promotors were eager to depict the Skyline route as an experience open to a broad audience of outdoor recreationists, not just rugged outdoorsmen. Nothing exemplified this trend more than the increasing number of women traveling on the trail by the late 1920s.

## A "Feminine Trend" on the Skyline

In the late nineteenth century, outdoor recreation was still mainly viewed as a gendered experience. However, that began to change as outdoor groups like the Seattle Mountaineers and the Mazamas welcomed women into their ranks. Women were among the charter members and leadership of both organizations and were welcomed on club outings. By the 1920s, the Mazamas had brought hundreds of women on their annual trips into the High Cascades.

But beyond the Mazamas, only a few other women had spent considerable time on the Skyline route. One of them was Connie Bingham, who spent five seasons with her forest ranger husband, Cy, during his extended patrols in the Cascades. Cy and Connie met in Austin, Washington. They spent their first years of marriage riding between mining camps in Idaho, eastern Oregon and Bohemia City, now a ghost town in the Cascade foothills, deep inside the Umpqua National Forest.

When Cy began working for the General Land Office in 1903, Connie spent several years with him on the trail. Cy called her a "calico cowboy," who was at home in the saddle, "even with a skirt on." Connie had her own shotgun and tracked game while Cy worked the trails during the day. She could hunt and fish as well as any ranger. Connie skinned and tanned the hides from her hunts to make camp rugs.[262] By the time Cy left the Cascades to become forest supervisor of the Malheur National Forest, Connie had probably spent more time on the Skyline route than any other woman in Oregon.

Margie Young Knowles was another ranger spouse who spent several years on the trail. She and her husband, Archie Knowles, were originally from the Siuslaw River Valley, around the present-day site of Mapleton. The couple met at the gold mining camp in Bohemia in 1906.[263] Margie's father had been the first forest ranger in the Siuslaw area, so she was familiar with the hardships of life on the trail. In the summer of 1908, Archie was hired by the Forest Service and assigned to work the eastern side of the crest, based out of Davis Lake.[264]

Archie's new job began on the day after their wedding, and the couple left for the Cascades the next morning. Margie left Mapleton on a horse named Pet, using her grandfather's old McClellan saddle from the Civil War. Although automobiles were starting to be seen around Oregon, in that day a ranger's work was still done on horseback. When she was on the trail, Margie rode with a 25-20 Winchester rifle, a bedroll, and some oats for the horses.

Like Connie Bingham, Margie did most of the camp work while Archie was out on his ranger duties. But she often traveled with him on the trail, including frequent 25-mile trips to Roseland, an old post office site located a few miles north of present-day La Pine. Every other week, Archie and Margie would ride to Roseland to pick up mail and supplies. Margie guessed she covered 1,500 miles on horseback during their first season in the High Cascades.[265]

A ranger's season typically lasted from June until late October when the snow returned to the Cascades. At the end of their first summer, Archie and

Margie struggled to leave the mountains through two feet of snow as they left Odell Lake to spend winter in Eugene. Margie appropriately titled her later autobiography *Honeymoon on Horseback*.

In 1909, the Forest Service transferred Archie to Cascadia, where he worked in the Western Cascades along the South Santiam River. At the time, the district was part of the Cascade National Forest, which became part of the Willamette National Forest in 1933. The couple spent the first four years of their marriage in the Cascades before settling down. Although the work was never easy, Margie remembered her years on the trail as a "glorious adventure."[266]

However exciting, the experiences that Connie and Margie had on the trail were very different from what was desired by casual recreationists of the 1920s. Organized Mazama outings and Eugene Dowling's pack trips offered a more accessible way to experience the trail. This more relaxed style of outdoor recreation invited women into spaces previously reserved for men.

One bizarre story appearing in the *Bend Bulletin* from 1922 even suggested that a new "feminine trend" was emerging on the Skyline, evidenced by a sampling of trash found along the path. That year, a Forest Service grazing

Female members of the Obsidians during a club outing along the Skyline Trail, 1934. *Special Collections & University Archives, University of Oregon.*

examiner covering the route between Crescent and Odell Lakes reported finding an increasing number of chocolate and gum wrappers along the trail. This trash was replacing the traditional trailside detritus of tobacco containers and cigarette paper. The grazing examiner interpreted this new type of litter as evidence that the Skyline trail was "being used more and more by parties composed largely of women."[267] Although his logic was faulty, it was true that female travelers were a more common sight along the Skyline by the late 1920s.

At the time, most of the women were part of larger outings. Solo travel by female adventurers was still rare enough to draw attention from the media. In 1933, a young Portland woman named Jacqueline Arte made the entire trip along the trail by horseback. Her six-month journey included numerous side trips down the feeder trails, taking her places "seldom visited by man and perhaps never before by woman."[268] Over six months, she rode and hiked nearly two thousand miles of trails between Government Camp and Crater Lake on a horse named Red Wing. During the journey, she reportedly wore out two pairs of riding boots and another two pairs of oxfords.

## TRAILS BEYOND THE SKYLINE

The idea for the Skyline Trail did not evolve in isolation. It came at a time when outdoor clubs on both coasts were developing other long-distance hiking trails. One year to the day after Frederick Cleator finished his Skyline survey, Benton MacKaye published an article in the *Journal of the American Institute of Architects* presenting his idea for the Appalachian Trail.[269]

MacKaye's vision for the Appalachian Trail was starkly different from what Cleator and the Forest Service had in mind for the Cascades. The Appalachian Trail was as much a sociological experiment as it was a recreational trail. The idea was embedded within MacKaye's theories about community planning in response to societal problems created by capitalism, urbanization and rapid technological change.[270] MacKaye hoped that the Appalachian Trail and a series of "community camps" along its path would offer "a new approach to the problem of living."

The camp communities along the trail would be engaged in nonindustrial activity, offering "a refuge from the scramble of everyday worldly commercial life…[and] a retreat from profit.[271] Like Aldo Leopold,

MacKaye was concerned about the impact of road development and automobiles on isolated wilderness. He intended the Appalachian Trail as a path for walking, separate and distinct from the emerging culture of the automobile.[272]

There were other significant differences between the two trails. Much of the initial support for the Skyline route came from Oregon's tourism and automobile lobbies. Conversely, the Appalachian Trail evolved as a grassroots movement supported by community trail clubs and hiking enthusiasts.[273] When MacKaye presented his proposal, about a third of the path already existed as segments of regional trails developed over the years by community hiking clubs in New England and New York. Those groups responded enthusiastically to MacKaye's proposal and worked to link the segments into a single trail stretching from Georgia to Maine.

Another difference between the two trails was the government's role in their development. The Skyline Trail was, first and foremost, a Forest Service initiative. Although local boosters supported it, the Forest Service led its planning, surveying and development. Conversely, there was much less government involvement in the early stages of the Appalachian Trail.

As the route matured, the Forest Service became more involved in developing sections of the Appalachian Trail where it passed through the national forests.[274] This was particularly true after 1938 with the Appalachian Trailway Agreement between the National Park Service, the Forest Service and the Appalachian Trail Conservancy.[275] That agreement created a narrow, protected strip of land on either side of the Appalachian Trail and enlisted government support in developing shelters and securing easements along the route.

One commonality between the trails was how the rise of automobile culture profoundly influenced their development. By the 1930s, there were increasing concerns about the encroachment of automobiles along both routes. The Roosevelt administration had proposed a new road running parallel to a section of the Appalachian Trail passing through the Shenandoah National Park in Virginia. The 105-mile route, known as "Skyline Drive," threatened to destroy a scenic section of the trail along the crest of the Blue Ridge Mountains.

Benton MacKaye lobbied vigorously against the Skyline Drive, arguing that "the Appalachian Trail is a wilderness trail, or it is nothing."[276] The controversy led to an infamous break between MacKaye and Myron Avery, chairman of the Appalachian Trail Conference (ATC). Ultimately, Avery and the ATC opted to work with the federal government and reroute nearly

Benton MacKaye (*left*) proposed the idea for the Appalachian Trail in the fall of 1921 and later helped establish the Wilderness Society in 1935. Myron Avery (*right*) was responsible for overseeing the trail's completion during the 1930s as chairman of the Appalachian Trail Conference. *Courtesy of the Appalachian Trail Conservancy.*

120 miles of the Appalachian Trail to make way for Skyline Drive. Avery would later regret that compromise, calling it "the major catastrophe in Appalachian Trail history."[277]

Oregon's Skyline Trail and the Appalachian Trail were not the only long-distance hiking paths under development at the time. During the 1920s, work was also underway on the John Muir Trail in California and the Cascade Crest Trail in Washington. Washington's Cascade Crest Trail began in the early twentieth century, evolving from a trail system established by the Seattle Mountaineers around the club's camp near Snoqualmie Pass.[278]

Pacific Crest Trail historian Barney Mann credits schoolteacher Catherine Montgomery with first suggesting turning Washington's trail system into an extended route stretching from Canada to Mexico.[279] Montgomery lived in Bellingham and was an avid hiker. In 1926, she met Seattle Mountaineer Joseph Hazard and suggested the idea of a border-to-border trail. Hazard later recalled that conversation in his 1946 book, *Pacific Crest Trails.*

Catherine Montgomery
was an educator and
hiker from Bellingham,
Washington. She is known
as the "Mother of the
Pacific Crest Trail" for
first suggesting the idea of
a border-to-border trail
stretching from Canada
to Mexico. *Courtesy of the
Washington State Parks and
Recreation Commission.*

Hazard reportedly took Montgomery's idea and presented the plan to
the local hiking club in Bellingham. It spread from there to other outdoor
groups. With the help of the Forest Service, the project gradually became
the Washington portion of the Pacific Crest Trail, connecting to the Skyline
Trail at the Bridge of the Gods, spanning the Columbia River. Today,
Montgomery is remembered as the "Mother of the Pacific Crest Trail."

By the 1920s, there were segments of several other long-distance hiking
trails in California, including the Tahoe-Yosemite and John Muir trails. The
Forest Service began developing the 185-mile Tahoe-Yosemite Trail in 1916,
connecting Lake Tahoe with the northern boundary of Yosemite National
Park. Meanwhile, the National Park Service worked on the section of the
route from Yosemite Valley to Tuolumne Meadows, connecting it to the
John Muir Trail.

Like the Skyline Trail, portions of the 211-mile John Muir Trail had a
prehistory as an Indigenous footpath used for hunting and trade along the

Sierra. Theodore Solomons, an early member of the Sierra Club, is credited with first exploring and proposing a long trail through the High Sierra. In the early twentieth century, Joseph LeConte, James Hutchinson and Duncan McDuffie scouted a trail from Yosemite National Park to Kings Canyon, blazing something close to the eventual route of the John Muir Trail.

In 1914, the Sierra Club began working with the State of California to develop that trail. Construction began the following year. After the unexpected death of Sierra Club president John Muir in 1914, fellow club members lobbied to have the trail named in his honor. The JMT route was nearly complete by the late 1920s, but work on several challenging sections continued into the 1930s as a joint effort by the Forest Service and the National Park Service. The various trail sections in California, Washington and Oregon would comprise the Pacific Crest Trail when linked in the late 1930s.

## A Skyline Reimagined

By the end of the 1920s, the Skyline Trail was no closer to becoming a scenic highway than it was when Cleator made his survey a decade earlier. The stock market crash and the Great Depression ended any hope of completing the extravagant engineering project. Although the road boosters never achieved their ambitions, the trail had acquired a certain mystique by remaining a primitive footpath. It inspired works of art, novels and poetry and was the subject of countless photographs and drawings. The name was even adopted by Bend's famous ski club, known as the Skyliners.[280]

Bend Skyliners ski club logo. Skyliners club member Paul Hosmer won a contest for proposing the club's name in 1927. *Deschutes County Historical Society.*

In 1924, Mary Carolyn Davies wrote a book of poetry inspired by the trail. Davies had moved to Portland as a child, graduating from Washington High School in 1910. She briefly taught school in Central Oregon before attending the University of California at Berkeley and later moved to New York City to pursue poetry and playwriting.[281] She became the first woman to win the Bohemian Club Prize for poetry.

*Left*: Celebrated poet Mary Carolyn Davies of Portland, author of *The Skyline Trail*. *Oregon State University Special Collections and Archives Research Center*.

*Below*: A pack train on the Skyline Trail near Scott Camp with Middle Sister in the background, early 1930s. *Photograph by Frederick Cleator. Forest History Society*.

Davies's poetry collection, titled *The Skyline Trail*, celebrated the western landscapes where she was raised. One reviewer wrote that Davies's book "sings of the West, of Oregon, of the lure of high places of the mountain trail... redolent with scents of Oregon forests, of the perfume of pine and fur [*sic*]."[282]

The Skyline Trail had many admirers, but it never captured the popular imagination as its backers had hoped. A 1930 article in the *Oregonian* noted a "singular lack of local interest in the splendid Skyline Trail," noting that only a few Oregonians were willing to make such a trek.[283] One Forest Service official lamented that the trail was "perhaps better known in the East than it is to Oregonians."[284] Nevertheless, the *Oregonian* held on to the hopes of the route's early boosters, predicting that future years would "see the Skyline trail in high favor with tourists."[285]

By 1931, when the Forest Service released an updated trail map, it was clear that the agency had all but abandoned the idea of a scenic highway. Unlike the 1921 version, the new trail map made no mention of the Skyline Road, suggesting that the agency had come to view it strictly as a nonmotorized recreational trail. Furthermore, the newspaper accounts about the new map said nothing about the proposed road. That was a far cry from the vocal boosterism of the early 1920s when Oregon's major papers celebrated the Skyline Road idea unabashedly.

Historian Stuart Barker suggested that several factors were behind the waning interest. The most crucial issue was simply the impracticality of a high alpine road. The realities of challenging engineering, exorbitant cost and a short season of use likely made the road infeasible. A second factor undermining the trail's popularity was that the Skyline experience was out of sync with the public's changing recreational preferences. By the 1930s, even Cleator felt the trail was too arduous for the average tourist.[286]

Despite fading enthusiasm, the 1930s would bring an unexpected boost to the trail's prospects. In response to the Great Depression, Franklin Delano Roosevelt announced plans in early 1933 to create what he called a "conservation army," putting unemployed young men back to work on the nation's public lands. As part of the New Deal, the Civilian Conservation Corps (CCC) undertook hundreds of recreational infrastructure projects around the country. In Oregon, these included iconic landmarks like Timberline Lodge and Silver Falls State Park. Hundreds of young men assigned to CCC camps in the Cascades worked along the Skyline Trail route, presenting a unique opportunity to refine the trail's rough edges and reimagine its purpose.

# 6

# REINVENTING THE SKYLINE

## *The New Deal and the Pacific Crest Trail*

By the end of the 1920s, there had been little progress on turning the Skyline Trail into a scenic highway. Several sections of forest road adjacent to the trail's length had been improved for automobiles, but not along Cleator's route. New road sections included the Lost Lake Highway connecting Hood River to Lost Lake, Century Drive between Elk and Lava Lakes and improved routes linking Crater Lake to the area around Willamette Pass. But with the economic turmoil of the Great Depression, the Forest Service lost enthusiasm for expensive development projects.

After the stock market crash of 1929, the government greatly reduced funding for Forest Service recreation and infrastructure development.[287] When President Roosevelt took office in March 1933, around 25 percent of the country's labor force was unemployed. But the dire economic crisis delivered an unexpected silver lining for the Skyline Trail. As the Roosevelt administration developed its response to the Depression, the Forest Service played a vital role in putting unemployed Americans back to work. Those programs brought a surge of funding and labor for projects along the Skyline Trail during the mid-1930s.

In April 1933, the Forest Service published a 1,677-page document titled *A National Plan for American Forestry*, also known as the Copeland Report. It was a comprehensive study of American forestry practices covering timber, water, range, wildlife, fire protection and recreation. The Copeland Report became the blueprint for how the Roosevelt administration approached forestry within the context of its New Deal recovery programs.[288]

The Copeland Report called for an intensive forest management program as the country was suffering massive unemployment. The Roosevelt administration saw forestry as one way of getting Americans back to work while achieving another goal of revitalizing public lands. New Deal forestry programs raised the stature of recreation among the agency's many responsibilities. The Copeland Report had an entire chapter dedicated to outdoor recreation, written by Bob Marshall, a young forester and conservationist.

Marshall was known in the Forest Service for his field research in Montana and Alaska during the 1920s and made numerous trips to Oregon. His first Forest Service job in 1924 was an internship in Carson, Washington, along the Columbia River Gorge. He capped off his summer by summiting Mount Hood before returning East to complete a master's degree in forestry at Harvard.

During the mid-1930s, while serving as the director of forestry in the Bureau of Indian Affairs, Marshall visited the Klamath Agency and Warm Springs Reservation. He also made tours of Oregon's national forests while serving in Washington, D.C., as the director of the Forest Service's Recreation and Lands division. Between those endeavors, Marshall earned a doctorate in forestry from Johns Hopkins University and published a best-selling book about his time living among Alaska Natives in the Brooks Range.

Among all his achievements, Marshall was perhaps most famous for his 1930 essay "The Problem of the Wilderness," arguing for the physical, mental and esthetic benefits of preserving wilderness areas.[289] The article is widely credited with creating the early momentum for the wilderness preservation movement during the 1930s.

Marshall's chapter of the Copeland Report noted that recreation on forest lands was "growing with tremendous acceleration" and needed to be managed accordingly.[290] He argued that forests were becoming a vital "escape from civilization" for American citizens and called for developing trails, campgrounds and recreational areas to satisfy the growing need. Amid the Great Depression, Americans viewed forest lands as an affordable escape for recreation, leisure and enjoyment. Between 1933 and 1940, annual visitation in the national forests increased from 8 to 20 million.[291]

The Copeland Report offered the Roosevelt administration a roadmap for getting thousands of Americans back to work through an unprecedented investment in public lands. Many of these plans involved conservation and recreation projects under the auspices of the Civilian Conservation Corps (CCC). Despite the state's small population, Oregon had one of the highest

Bob Marshall, date unknown. The Bancroft Library, University of California, Berkeley.

numbers of CCC camps in the nation.[292] Nearly half of the fifty-one CCC camps around the state were inside the national forests.

In Oregon and across the western United States, the CCC undertook hundreds of projects to develop recreational infrastructure, including campgrounds, lodges, trail systems and ski resorts. In the Cascades, projects included efforts to reroute sections of the Skyline Trail and improve amenities along the route. New Deal works programs provided an unexpected source of funding and labor, enabling the Forest Service to reimagine the Skyline Trail, turning it into something far different from its original concept.

## THE CCC GOES TO WORK IN OREGON'S FORESTS

In early April 1933, President Roosevelt established the CCC by executive order. The U.S. Army initially organized the camps and managed the recruits. By the end of the summer, there were around 1,400 camps across the country, with more than 250,000 young men enrolled. The men signed up for an initial period of six months at the rate of one dollar per day, with an option of working a maximum term of two years.[293] Room, board, clothing and transportation were provided.

Vancouver Barracks along the Columbia River became the CCC's regional headquarters for the Pacific Northwest. By August 1933, almost thirteen thousand men were assigned to forty-eight camps around Oregon.[294] Additionally, there were numerous "side camps" scattered throughout the Cascades. These were smaller, temporary camps at remote work locations, consisting of ten to twenty men living in tents, with a foreman in charge.[295] Since most of the enlistees came from outside the state, they worked under the leadership of "local experienced men" like Dee Wright, hired to manage the crews.

Around twenty of the state's CCC camps fell under Forest Service supervision. Most of those camps were in the Mount Hood and Willamette National Forests.[296] Several camps around Mount Hood were located at Zigzag and Cascade Locks. The Willamette National Forest hosted larger camps at Belknap, near McKenzie Bridge; at Oakridge, near the Pope and Talbot mill; at Fall Creek, near Lowell; and Cascadia, near the junction of Canyon Creek and the Santiam River.[297] Other smaller camps were located at Fish Lake, Humbug Creek, Seven Mile Hill, Snow Creek, Bear Pass and other sites.

At first, the CCC crews focused on traditional forestry duties such as tree planting, roadbuilding, timber thinning, erosion control and firefighting. Many early road and trail projects were built for fire control but later repurposed for recreational use. These included the road connecting Olallie

A CCC trail crew with Ranger Roy Elliott in the Willamette National Forest, 1933. Photograph by Frederick Cleator. *Oregon State University Special Collections and Archives Research Center.*

Mealtime at the CCC Camp Belknap near McKenzie Bridge, 1933. *U.S. Forest Service.*

The "Spirit of CCC" by Forest Service illustrator Harry Rossoll, 1938. Rossoll later gained fame as one of the creators of the Smokey Bear campaign to prevent forest fires. *Courtesy of CCC Legacy.*

Lake with the Breitenbush Hot Springs and the Timberline Loop Trail around Mount Hood.[298]

As the CCC program evolved, the Forest Service began including more projects focused on recreation. Under Chief Forester Ferdinand Silcox, the agency's administrative regions were given autonomy to pursue recreational development appropriate to each area. Silcox wanted the Forest Service to emphasize forestry's "social" aspects, which meant developing facilities like campgrounds, shelters, resorts and recreational areas.[299]

Around 25 percent of the CCC projects in the Willamette National Forest focused on recreation.[300] Most of the work projects were meant to be simple and inexpensive. But they also included ambitious projects like Timberline Lodge on Mount Hood, funded by the Works Progress Administration (WPA).

In 1928, Frederick Cleator was named recreation supervisor for the Pacific Northwest. By that point in his career, he was arguably the most experienced recreation specialist in the entire Forest Service, supervising a region known for such programs.[301] At the time, areas like Eagle Creek Campground, McKenzie Bridge and Mount Hood were some of the most popular recreational areas in the country. Bob Marshall commended

CCC workers constructing campground stoves in the Siskiyou National Forest. *U.S. Forest Service.*

The Timberline Lodge at Mount Hood was one of the most ambitious recreational infrastructure projects of the New Deal era. *Oregon Explorer, Oregon State University.*

Cleator's work in making the Pacific Northwest the leading region in the nation for recreational planning.[302]

As the regional supervisor for recreation, Cleator oversaw many of the projects done by the CCC during the New Deal years. With the surge of funding and labor for recreational development, Cleator was prepared with a list of projects to improve the Skyline Trail. By that time, he understood that the Skyline route would never become a scenic highway. The project was too ambitious, overly expensive and didn't fit into the Forest Service's evolving priorities. The next phase of the Skyline's evolution would focus on making the trail more accessible to general users.

By the end of the 1920s, the Skyline route was still underutilized, except by hardy adventurers who were comfortable navigating a primitive backcountry trail with few amenities. Cleator hoped to broaden the trail's appeal with improvements such as better routing, improved signage and shelters to make the path accessible to ordinary hikers.[303] That vision informed much of the work undertaken by CCC crews during the mid-1930s. Work began almost as soon as the CCC camps opened during the summer of 1933. Projects included rerouting difficult trail sections and building shortcuts that considerably reduced the trail's overall length.

One of the early projects involved moving a sizable section of the trail over McKenzie Pass between White Branch Creek and Big Lake. The task involved rerouting the trail where it crossed the old McKenzie Highway near Frog Camp. The new route tracked around to Collier Glacier, passing by Mathieu Lakes and crossing the highway closer to the crest line. From there, the trail cut east around Belknap Crater before continuing to Mount Washington and Big Lake.[304] The new trail was much closer to what Cleator had originally envisioned for that section of the route during his 1920 survey.

Cleator also wanted to develop a series of shelters along the Skyline Trail. The shelters had been part of his initial plan during the 1920s; however, only a few had been built in the intervening years. The windfall of funding and labor from the New Deal programs provided an opportunity to build more.[305] The shelters were constructed in an Adirondack style, giving them a primitive, rustic appearance. They had an open-front design and were made of local timber, avoiding the need to bring in construction materials. The roofs and walls were made of wood shakes made on-site and by hand.

Work on the first shelter began in the spring of 1933. It became known as the Sunshine Shelter, located near Frog Camp, northwest of the Three Sisters. Over the next several years, CCC crews built additional shelters at

A CCC crew working on a Skyline Trail shelter near the south fork of White Branch Creek, July 1934. *Photo by Frederick Cleator. U.S. Forest Service.*

popular locations along the trail, including Mink Lake, Irish Lake, Charlton Lake and South Waldo Lake.[306]

Crews also worked to fix difficult sections of the trail, improving accessibility and connections to nearby recreation areas. New shortcuts and rerouting reduced the trail's distance between Mount Hood and Crater Lake by about fifty miles.[307] Cleator hoped these improvements would make the route more inviting to average users.

In the summer of 1933, Cleator publicly declared the Skyline Trail completed from Crater Lake to Mount Hood.[308] But in truth, work on the Skyline Trail never ended. The following year, he sent forester William Royer out on a new survey to identify areas for additional improvements. Trail work during the 1930s became a process of continual refinement with the goal of making "the trail safe, useable, and convenient to any ordinary hiker."[309]

## DEE WRIGHT: A LIFE SPENT ON THE SKYLINE

During the depths of the Great Depression, Dee Wright served as one of the CCC's "local experienced men" overseeing the crews working along the Skyline Trail. By then, Wright had spent decades in the High Cascades. He began his Forest Service career in 1910, working on both the Mount Hood and later the Willamette National Forests. His time with the CCC would become the symbolic bookend of a life lived along the Skyline.

In 1932, the Forest Service directed Wright to reroute a section of the Skyline Trail between Mount Washington and the Three Sisters. Ironically, when Cleator scouted that section of the trail during the 1920 survey, he followed the path that Dee Wright and Henry Yelkus had taken during the summer of 1891. That route went far to the west of Mount Washington and Belknap Crater, avoiding some of the treacherous lava fields around McKenzie Pass.

Cleator felt that the section was the "most difficult along the entire route" for trail building.[310] Despite the terrain challenges, Cleator preferred a path closer to the summit, along the eastern side of Belknap Crater. However, to keep the project within budget, he opted for an easier route, closer to the one used by Wright and Yelkus in 1891. But by the early 1930s, with the highway plan abandoned, the Forest Service took the opportunity to reroute the trail closer to Cleator's original intent, affording better views of the High Desert to the East.

*Above*: A view of McKenzie Pass summit shortly before the rerouting of the Skyline Trail and construction of the Dee Wright Observatory, 1930. *US Forest Service.*

*Left*: Government packer Dee Wright posting a Skyline Trail sign, 1931. *U.S. Forest Service.*

The new route passed by Little Brother before veering east along a section of the old Scott Trail, past Yapoah Crater, Mathieu Lakes and Lava Camp. It crossed the McKenzie Highway near the summit before tracking around to the east of Belknap Crater.[311] Dee Wright personally scouted the new route and supervised its construction.

In the fall of 1932, the *Bend Bulletin* reported enthusiastically on Wright's progress, offering "praise and congratulations for a well-planned job."[312] The paper noted that Wright's work added "many miles of actual skyline to

A CCC crew building what will become the Dee Wright Observatory, named in Wright's honor after he died working on the Skyline Trail in 1934. *U.S. Forest Service.*

the Skyline Trail." It showered admiration on Wright's thoughtful trail work, calling it "something that hits you in the eye." The article predicted that "as time passes, it will become a famous section of the Skyline."

By the summer of 1934, Wright was leading a CCC crew working on the northern section of the project from the McKenzie Highway through the lava fields around Belknap Crater, past Mount Washington to Big Lake.[313] Unfortunately, Wright never got to complete that section of his project. In the spring of 1934, he suffered a fatal heart attack while rowing his crew across the McKenzie River near the CCC camp at Belknap Springs.[314]

The news of Wright's death shocked those who knew him as a fixture on the trail. As word spread, he was immortalized on the pages of several Oregon newspapers. The *Portland Journal* dramatically announced that "Dee Wright of the high Cascade trails has fallen abruptly as do the oldest, tallest trees."[315] The *Bend Bulletin* penned a fitting obituary, describing Wright as "a skilled woodsman, a first-grade mountain trail maker, and the man best acquainted with the high country of the Cascades from Mount Hood to Crater Lake."[316]

At the time of Wright's death, another CCC crew was constructing a mountain observatory near where the rerouted Skyline Trail crossed the McKenzie Highway. The structure was built from blocks of basaltic andesite lava taken from the site of the Yapoah Cone eruption some two thousand years before and offered panoramic views of the Central Cascades. When the crew completed the observatory in 1935, it was named in Wright's honor. At the time of Dee Wright's death, few, if any, living Oregonians had spent as much time on the Skyline Trail.

## THE ROYER RECONNAISSANCE

As the CCC began its work in the Cascades, Cleator tasked forester William Royer with surveying the conditions along the Skyline Trail to determine a plan for future work. Royer was an assistant forestry technician for the Mount Hood National Forest and was familiar with the Cascades. His instructions were to identify areas for improvements along the route, making it safer and more accessible for recreation.[317]

Like his ranger predecessors, Cy Bingham and Archie Knowles, Royer's wife accompanied him for much of the journey between Breitenbush and Crater Lake.[318] They began their travels in late July 1934 with two saddle

A CCC crew working on the Skyline Trail in the Umpqua National Forest. *U.S. Forest Service.*

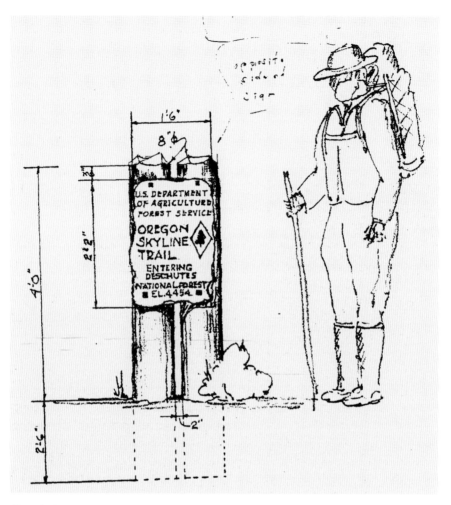

*Above*: A sketch of the proposed Skyline Trail boundary sign for the Deschutes National Forest, July 1938. *U.S. Forest Service.*

*Opposite*: The cover image of the Oregon Skyline Trail map, 1936. *Oregon Historical Society.*

horses and a pack animal. The survey started in mid-July with a plan to finish at Crater Lake by the end of summer. His assigned section represented the heart of the Skyline Trail. At the same time, work was underway to integrate newer sections of the trail from the Columbia River to Mount Hood in the north and from Crater Lake to the California border in the south.[319]

Another important objective was to improve trail access points to accommodate hikers and riders wishing to explore shorter sections of the

OREGON
SKYLINE TRAIL
1936

PACIFIC
CREST SYSTEM
U. S. DEPT. OF AGRICULTURE
FOREST SERVICE
REGION-6
GUIDE NO. 35 OREGON

route. This change would also offer better access to resupply for those traveling the entire trail length. Cleator and Royer hoped to strike a balance for trail users with these improvements. They wanted to "modernize the conveniences to make it a comfortable excursion for even the most city wise" but at the same time maintain "its rugged state where possible to satisfy those travelers searching for the primitive."[320]

After completing the survey, Royer spent the autumn compiling a detailed trip report covering the trail conditions and areas that still needed "polishing." His final report included recommendations for minor rerouting around hazardous areas, evaluation of campsites, proposed locations for new shelters and restrooms and plans for improved signage. Royer's work offered a slate of new projects for the CCC crews. The Forest Service eventually hoped to build as many as 150 shelters along the trail and a similar number of campgrounds.[321]

Royer's trip report offered other interesting details about his journey along the Skyline. He traveled 330 miles over the summer, including thirty-one days on horseback. Along the way, he spotted forty-one species of birds, mostly juncos, jays and chickadees. Royer also noted an abundance of deer and elk along the route, along with some sheep. He spotted bear tracks along the route; however, he didn't see the animals themselves.

One of Royer's comments provided an interesting observation about the bureaucratic disconnect between the Forest Service and the Park Service. Royer had difficulty following the trail around Crater Lake as he traveled through the park. He noted an absence of signage marking the path and observed that the route didn't appear on any park maps. When Royer questioned park officials about the situation, they claimed they were unaware of the trail's existence.[322] By the late 1930s, the situation had been resolved, as the Park Service completed its section of the Skyline Trail through Crater Lake National Park and added appropriate signage.

In the report's closing comments, Royer noted that the trail was nearing completion but still needed some "final polishing." Nevertheless, he was confident in the project's potential, noting that "in a very few years, the ideal will be realized when, over more than 350 miles of good trail, through and above the finest mountain scenery, the Oregon Skyline Trail will reach from the Columbia River south to the state of California."[323]

## Preserving and Protecting the Skyline: Bob Marshall's Vision for Wilderness Protection

Bob Marshall's chapter on recreation in the 1933 Copeland Report provided a blueprint for how the Forest Service approached recreation development during the New Deal era. It helped justify a significant expansion of recreation infrastructure on public lands. Most of these projects were low-cost, basic designs and ready-made for the labor of young CCC crews. Nevertheless, these projects left a lasting imprint on Oregon's forests. By the end of the 1930s, Oregon had over five hundred new campgrounds. California was the only state in the union with more such facilities.[324]

Many of the projects were small recreational sites, but they also included complex endeavors like the Timberline Lodge, constructed between 1936 and 1938 and funded by the Works Progress Administration. That project employed hundreds of skilled artisans who built the forty-thousand-square-foot lodge using local materials. President and Eleanor Roosevelt dedicated the lodge in person on September 28, 1937, making it one of the iconic structures of the New Deal era.

Timberline Lodge represented the high-water mark of the Forest Service's recreational development of the 1930s. After that, the agency experienced a gradual decrease in funding and personnel. CCC enrollment peaked at around half a million men in 1935 and declined steadily afterward. Following five years of rapid growth, the late 1930s brought about a period of more limited ambitions. Nevertheless, the agency's recreational program grew in stature in May 1937 when Bob Marshall was appointed chief of recreation and lands.

During his brief career, Marshall worked tirelessly to expand recreational opportunities on public lands, especially for minorities and lower-income Americans.[325] In 1936, he wrote to Forest Service chief Ferdinand Silcox that he viewed recreation "fully as important and valid use of the national forests as is timber cutting. I believe it can be demonstrated that more people have materially benefitted each year from national forests for recreation than from the use of national forests for lumber."[326]

Marshall's tenure marked a transition in how the Forest Service approached recreational development. The agency had emphasized physical infrastructure during the 1920s and the early New Deal period, building thousands of campsites, shelters, resorts, residential tracts, picnic areas, forest roads and trails. During that time, recreation foresters like Frederick Cleator left an indelible legacy on Oregon's forests through such projects.

While Marshall was a strong advocate for recreation, he was also wary about some of the agency's development projects in the forests. By the mid-1930s, he had become increasingly disenchanted with the CCC's extensive roadbuilding projects that were cutting vast swaths through previously untouched wilderness.[327] He was particularly concerned about the Corps' plans to build "skyline" roads through the Great Smoky Mountains and other areas.

In 1935, Marshall founded and endowed the Wilderness Society, which became one of the nation's leading conservation organizations advocating for wilderness preservation. Through his advocacy inside and outside the agency, Marshall pressed the Forest Service to place more emphasis on safeguarding wilderness areas and less on developing physical infrastructure in the forests.

Like his fellow forester Aldo Leopold, Marshall was particularly concerned about the impact of automobiles on natural areas. He wrote that "the sounds of the forest are entirely obliterated by the roar of the motor. The smell of pine needles and flowers and herbs and freshly turned dirt and all the other delicate odors of the forest are drowned in the stench of gasoline."[328] In the Copeland Report, Marshall had argued for the importance of preserving some recreation areas in their natural state without modification by man.[329]

In the same report, Marshall offered a working definition of "wilderness areas," which he viewed as a space without permanent inhabitants and mechanical conveyance. For such areas, Marshall recommended a prohibition of all roads, settlements and power transportation. Only trails and temporary shelters would be allowed. Marshall acknowledged that such areas would likely be limited to "sections of high mountain country where commercial values are low."[330] However, many of the CCC's projects in Oregon were moving in the opposite direction by opening remote forests to development, logging and motorized traffic.

In 1935, Marshall wrote to Chief Forester Silcox, urging him to curtail CCC roadbuilding projects in the national forests, warning that "eager CCC boys will have demolished the greatest wildernesses which remain in the United States."[331] There's little doubt that Marshall's urgency to expand designated wilderness areas within Oregon's national forests was in response to the aggressive roadbuilding projects he saw happening out east. However, not everyone shared Marshall's zeal for limiting development in the national forests.

In Oregon, many state officials and members of the public supported the federal government's roadbuilding projects on public lands. A 1935 article from *Oregon Motorist* magazine summed up a common outlook, observing that roads in the national forests were opening "new worlds to conquer" for Oregonians, bringing the "recreational benefits of these forest assets much nearer home to the average citizen."[332]

By the mid-1930s, Marshall had refined and clarified his ideas about establishing protected wilderness. He considered tracts of at least 200,000 acres to be the minimal satisfactory size for a recreational wilderness. Marshall felt a great sense of urgency, warning that once roads were built into these areas, it would be difficult to restore them to wilderness. He thought that creating designated roadless areas was the only defense against an "invasion" of motorized vehicles.[333] Toward the end of the New Deal, Marshall pushed for the creation of dozens of new wilderness areas around the country while such lands still existed. The Forest Service and the public gradually came to understand and appreciate the value of what he proposed.

Before the Copeland Report, the Forest Service had established regulations giving the chief forester authority to designate tracts of undeveloped land as "Primitive Areas." The so-called L-20 regulations of 1929 limited the development of roads, buildings and formal recreational infrastructure within designated areas. However, these regulations didn't offer strong protection and they even allowed for limited logging and mining.[334] Nevertheless, the L-20 regulation was applied to several areas along the Skyline route. Among the very first to receive the designation was the Mount Jefferson Primitive Area in 1930, followed a year later by the Mount Hood Primitive Area.[335]

The Forest Service's views on primitive areas reflected the agency's changing perspective on outdoor recreation with a new emphasis on wilderness preservation.[336] Many of Oregon's outdoor groups strongly supported preserving 52,200 acres around Mount Jefferson. Three years later, the primitive area's size was more than doubled to include a large tract around Three Fingered Jack.[337] By that time, there was no longer any serious discussion about turning the Skyline Trail into an automobile route. Instead, the public's interest was slowly shifting in favor of preserving the invaluable wilderness areas surrounding the Skyline Trail.

Oregon's leading newspapers, once vocal boosters of the Skyline Road, came to appreciate the value of keeping the Skyline Trail as a protected wilderness footpath. In 1933, the Oregon chapter of the Izaak Walton League, a conservationist group of hunters and anglers, came out strongly against further development along the Skyline route.[338] By 1936, the Forest Service responded to these calls for preservation by prohibiting the use of motorized craft on several remote lakes along the trail, including Olallie and Breitenbush.[339]

Bob Marshall's brief tenure as director of recreation and lands marked a significant step forward in protecting the Cascades and other wilderness lands. One of his primary goals was expanding the number of such areas on National Forest System lands in the northwest region. Marshall was reportedly frustrated by Forest Service officials in Oregon and Washington, who he believed were too hesitant about nominating new areas for protection.[340] For that reason, Marshall became personally involved in the creation of the Three Sisters Primitive Area in 1937.[341]

On an inspection tour that year, Cleator escorted Marshall around Oregon and noted that his new boss came in with "a lot of steam and a lot of strong backing" for designating new wilderness areas.[342] Cleator reported that Marshall "insisted on throwing some kind of a boundary around every sizable piece of National Forest that didn't happen to have a road on it."[343] Marshall's approach apparently frustrated some regional officials. Cleator did his best to "keep peace in the family," although it put him in a difficult position. Cleator later claimed that he "understood his [Marshall's] dreams better than a lot of wood butchers did" and saw the value of protecting the wilderness areas adjacent to the Skyline route.[344]

The following year, Marshall pressed local officials to expand the Three Sisters Primitive Area boundary to include another fifty-five thousand acres encompassing the French Pete area west of Elk Lake and the Skyline Trail.[345] With Marshall's support, the Forest Service used its authority to reserve large sections of the Skyline Trail for recreational use. By 1937, this included almost the entire area around Mount Jefferson, Three Fingered Jack and the Three Sisters region. Between 1938 and 1944, all camps along the Skyline Trail were designated off-limits to sheep to reduce potential conflicts with recreational pack trains.[346] That decision represented a final nail in the coffin

Foresters Fred Asam, Frederick Cleator, Bob Marshall and John Seiker on the Umpqua National Forest, 1938. *Special Collections & University Archives, University of Oregon.*

of the controversy that had strained the friendship between Judge Waldo and John Minto during the 1890s.

In September 1939, Marshall made another inspection tour of the Pacific Northwest with stops in the Deschutes, Willamette and Umpqua National Forests. One of his main objectives was to identify additional tracts of undeveloped National Forest System lands in southwestern Oregon that could be designated as primitive areas.[347] This land included expansive, untouched stands of Douglas fir in the Umpqua and Willamette National Forests.[348] Sadly, this would be Marshall's last trip to Oregon.

Cleator was once again assigned to escort Marshall on the tour. During their time in the Willamette National Forest, Marshall was so taken by the scenery that he rode outside on the car's running boards to take it all in. While there, Marshall pressured regional Forest Service officials to move forward on establishing additional primitive areas along the Cascades.[349] During the tour, Cleator made a point of taking Marshall to Elk Lake to see the newly designated Three Sisters Primitive Area that he had fought for.[350]

While on the tour, Marshall received some good news from Washington, D.C., concerning a rule change that made the task of designating wilderness areas much easier. On September 19, Secretary of Agriculture Henry

Wallace signed a series of regulations written by Marshall, establishing stricter rules for protecting primitive areas in the national forests. The so-called U-Regulations strengthened the existing L-20 rules by prohibiting logging, road construction, resorts and summer homes inside designated wilderness areas. It also banned the use of motorized vehicles and limited recreational development by requiring special use permits to establish hotels, lodges, resorts and similar facilities.[351]

Cleator and Marshall continued the tour into Washington State, where they visited what is now the Wenatchee and Mount Baker-Snoqualmie National Forests. Cleator was familiar with the area from his previous assignments. Wenatchee was his first job as a young ranger, and in 1909, he did much of the forest's original boundary work.[352] In the late 1920s, while assigned in Washington, Cleator had blazed a wilderness trail from Darrington to Lake Chelan.

Marshall was known for maintaining a demanding work schedule, even when traveling. He often did thirty miles or more hiking per day during his inspection tours, as he did in the Umpqua National Forest earlier in the trip. While on the Wenatchee, he made one of his epic hikes before sharing a meal at a local restaurant with Cleator and the rest of the party. The following day, Marshall became violently ill and was hospitalized after experiencing convulsions. A few days later, he cut short the tour and returned to Washington, D.C.[353]

Once back home, Marshall resumed his busy work schedule, including another short inspection tour. Cleator was worried enough about Marshall's health to write him a short note, urging him to slow down a bit. Cleator fully expected to receive a reply of "mind your own business, Fred."[354] Instead, Marshall responded with a thoughtful note, thanking Cleator for the advice and for taking him on a "fine expedition" in Oregon and Washington. Marshall added, "I am only sorry that my stupid sickness prevented us from having three more days together, to which I had looked forward very much."[355] By the time Cleator received the letter, Marshall was dead.

In early November, Marshall had boarded an overnight train from Washington, D.C., to visit family in New York City. Sometime during the night, he died on the train, possibly from a heart attack. He was only thirty-eight years old and just two years into his tenure as the director of recreation and lands when he died. Nevertheless, his impact on the Forest Service and the conservation movement was enormous. During his short time with the agency, Marshall dramatically reshaped its policy on wilderness designation and recreation management.

But Marshall's most important legacy may have been his role as a co-founder of the Wilderness Society. The organization would become a driving force in the American conservation movement and instrumental in the passage of the Wilderness Act of 1964. That landmark legislation ensured that almost the entire length of the Skyline Trail would be protected within designated wilderness for perpetuity. The act established the framework for the creation of the Three Sisters, Mount Hood, Mount Washington and Diamond Peak Wildernesses in 1964; the Mount Jefferson Wilderness in 1968; and the Mount Thielsen and Waldo Lake Wildernesses in 1984.

## Integrating the Skyline into the Pacific Crest Trail System

The Skyline Road project initially sought to make the High Cascades accessible for a new age of auto tourism. The proposed scenic highway promised sightseers dramatic vistas through the windshield, with roadside picnic areas and drive-in campgrounds. But the exorbitant cost of roadbuilding killed the idea. By the early 1930s, the Skyline had been reincarnated as a wilderness footpath. With this new goal in mind, Cleator worked diligently to make the trail accessible to the average user, hoping to increase its popularity among the public. However, some trail supporters had other goals in mind and a different vision for the trail.

Although Cleator and Catherine Montgomery are credited with first proposing the idea for the Pacific Crest Trail, Clinton Clarke was the one who turned that vision into reality. During the early 1930s, Clarke was the chairman of the Mountain League of Los Angeles. In 1935, he organized the Pacific Crest Trail System Conference to promote the development of a long-distance hiking trail from Canada to Mexico.[356]

At the time of the conference, there were several existing segments of trail that Clarke wanted to link together into a contiguous route. They included the Cascade Crest Trail in Washington State and the Skyline Trail in Oregon. The Tahoe-Yosemite Trail and the John Muir Trail were already established in California. To fill in the remaining gaps, Clarke had plotted out two additional California segments that he dubbed the Lava Crest and the Desert Crest Trails.[357]

Before embarking on this endeavor, Clarke had been an investor and was active with the Boy Scouts. He saw the Pacific Crest Trail project as a vehicle

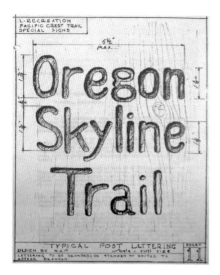

The proposed sign for the Oregon Skyline Trail section of the Pacific Crest Trail, circa 1936. *U.S. Forest Service.*

for building strong bodies, sound minds and patriotic citizens. Clarke differed significantly from Cleator regarding how he saw the trail being used and who would be on it. Clarke wrote that the Pacific Crest Trail was not intended to be "a recreational project for the casual camper or hiker."[358] In fact, he wanted exactly the opposite, urging that "the trail never be made popular for the average tourist type of recreation seeker." Instead, it should be reserved for "the true wilderness lover and nature worshipper."

Ironically, Clarke spent very little time on the trail during this lifetime and left the groundwork to others. Nevertheless, he was a skilled organizer who enlisted the help of numerous outdoor groups and government officials to bring the concept to fruition. The Pacific Crest Trail System Conference included representatives from the Boy Scouts, the YMCA, the Sierra Club, the California Alpine Club, the Mazamas of Portland, the Mountaineers of Seattle and the Federation of Western Outdoor Clubs.

Clarke expressed concerns with some of the CCC's recreation projects during the New Deal era. Nevertheless, he lobbied the Forest Service and Park Service for their help connecting existing trail segments and improving rough patches along the route. Clarke leveraged his close contacts with the YMCA and Boy Scouts to help survey the trail and identify areas needing refinement or rerouting.

As part of his effort to promote the trail, Clarke convinced the YMCA to organize teams of young hikers from across Washington, Oregon and California. Their task was to survey the route and report back on places where it still needed work. The relays began in June 1935 under the direction of YMCA organizer and trail legend Warren Rogers. Each group carried a logbook as they covered their assigned trail segments before handing it off to the next team. A total of forty teams covered the 2,300-mile route between the summers of 1935 and 1938.[359]

Eight groups of young men covered the Oregon section beginning in the summer of 1936, following the route of the Skyline Trail. Seven teams came from the Northeast Portland YMCA, making the city the largest single contributor of relay teams during the four-year effort.[360] The teams comprised two to five boys, aged fourteen to eighteen, accompanied by a trip leader. They carried all their gear in wood-framed Trapper Nelson packs that were used by the Boy Scouts from the 1930s through the 1960s. The teams were self-supported and carried all their food and supplies.

The first team left the Oregon-California border on August 23, 1936, and hiked for five days to Four-Mile Lake in the shadow of Mount McLoughlin.[361] There, they handed off the logbook to another team, which covered the next fifty-six miles to Crater Lake. A third team took over the section from Crater Lake to Odell Lake, finishing on September 5. After that, the relay took a hiatus for the season.

The relay continued the following summer, starting with a team from the Salem YMCA. They left Odell Lake on July 7, completing the first Oregon segment of 1937 and ending at Elk Lake. The next team continued to Big Lake near Santiam Pass. Gordon Petrie was a team member covering that section to Olallie Lake. Only two Oregon sections remained when Petrie's team reached the lake. But the next team was short a few boys, so Petrie agreed to join them to Mount Hood, extending his total trip to over one hundred miles.

Gordon Petrie leads one of the YMCA Relay teams across a meadow near Mowich Lake in the Mount Jefferson Wilderness, July 1937. From the collection of Gordon Petrie. *Courtesy of Barney Scout Mann.*

An original Pacific Crest Trail marker, approved by the Forest Service in 1937. *U.S. Forest Service.*

The final team took over at the Summit Guard station on Mount Hood and completed the last section to the Bridge of the Gods. At that point, they handed off the logbook to a fresh team from Washington. The reconnaissance for the Oregon section of the Pacific Crest Trail was completed by the end of July 1937. By the end of that summer, the Washington teams had made it to Stevens Pass. The remainder of the relay to Canada was completed the following year. Over four summers, the relay teams completed the entire length of the Pacific Crest Trail in 193 days.[362]

During the summer of 1937, the Forest Service approved the first official trail marker for the new Pacific Crest Trail. Forest Service employee W.J. Pollock designed the iconic diamond-shaped marker, which gradually replaced the rectangular metal signs posted by Cleator during the 1920 survey.[363] Although the original Skyline Trail had been integrated into the Pacific Crest Trail, the Forest Service continued to use the old Skyline name for signage along the Oregon section.

As work progressed, Clinton Clarke occasionally expressed frustration with the Forest Service for its slow pace and bureaucratic nature. But that frustration was sometimes mutual. Cleator later wrote that Clarke "kept my desk wall covered with correspondence and arguments, not only as to California but also infinite details of Oregon and Washington sections, with none of which he had much personal knowledge."[364] During a contentious debate over naming the trail, Cleator grew frustrated and wrote Clarke a terse note suggesting that it be called the "California - Oregon - Washington" trail, abbreviated as the COW Trail.[365] Cleator later confided that he regretted sending the flippant message on official Forest Service letterhead.

By the end of the 1930s, most of the trail in Oregon and Washington had been completed. However, there was still a good deal of work to be done connecting trail segments in California. At the time, a regional forester responsible for California described the route as "more of a myth than a trail."[366] Nevertheless, the Pacific Crest Trail was declared "passable" in 1937. Two years later, the trail began appearing on government maps for the first time. When completed, it measured 2,156 miles long from Canada to Mexico, passing through twenty-two national forests and five national parks.

## A SKYLINE REIMAGINED

Frederick Cleator continued to promote the Skyline Trail throughout the 1930s, long after the Forest Service abandoned the idea of a scenic highway. Cleator's subsequent writings suggested that he didn't regret the road's demise. He later claimed that even during the initial 1920 reconnaissance, all the survey members were against the road idea, believing that "coughing Fords and tin cans did not belong in this paradise."[367]

The Forest Service also engaged in some revisionist history regarding its original plan. By the end of the 1930s, there was hardly any mention of the scenic highway project. Instead, the Forest Service touted its clear foresight in preserving the primitive footpath for future generations, "where a lover of nature could always get entirely away from civilization and find a place to recreate himself in God's great outdoors."[368]

By the late 1930s, the Skyline Trail was much closer to what Cleator had first envisioned when he summited Diamond Peak in August 1920. On that day, he wrote in his diary, "I am beginning to think that a Skyline Trail the full length of the Cascades in Washington and Oregon, joining a similar trail in the Sierras of California, would be a great tourist advertisement....This is a future work, but it would be fine to plan upon."[369]

Cleator continued to promote its charms after the Skyline officially became part of the Pacific Crest Trail in the late 1930s. Cleator had taken hundreds of photographs along the trail over his twenty years developing recreation projects around Oregon. He often gave presentations to outdoor groups and led walks along sections of the route. One such event in Eugene marked the end of an era for the Skyline Trail.

On Friday, December 5, 1941, Cleator gave his Skyline Trail presentation to the Eugene Natural History Society. He discussed the remaining work to be done linking sections of the Skyline into the Pacific Crest Trail network through Washington and California. During the talk, Cleator revealed a bit of favoritism, reassuring his audience that "scenery is less beautiful" outside of Oregon.[370] The talk was followed by a walk along the McKenzie River scheduled for early Sunday morning. By the time the group returned from the hike, Oregonians were hearing the first reports of the Japanese attack on Pearl Harbor.

The war brought about dramatic changes for the Forest Service and the nation. It created an unprecedented demand for timber products after a decade of industry losses due to the Great Depression.[371] At the same time, many of the young men who were working at the CCC camps left for military service. By the time Congress formally terminated the CCC program in 1942, over eighty-five thousand young men had worked on various projects across Oregon.

There was a similarly dramatic change in recreational activity in the forests. During the war years, people had less time to enjoy activities like hiking, camping and skiing, which had been popularized during the 1930s. The Forest Service was preoccupied with supporting the war effort and temporarily ended its recreational planning and infrastructure development projects. Facilities like Timberline Lodge, ski areas and campgrounds around the state closed for the remainder of the war.

The Forest Service supported the war effort in various ways. When the War Production Board declared lumber a critical war material, there was an urgent need to protect Oregon's forests from wildfires. Due to concerns over incendiary attacks along the coast, aircraft warning stations were established in the national forests across California and the Pacific Northwest. Facing a labor shortage, the Forest Service employed older men, boys, women and conscientious objectors to fulfill the urgent need for timber workers and fire scouts.

The Forest Service also hosted military camps and training areas around the state. The Deschutes National Forest became the site of one of the largest training areas in Oregon, located at Camp Abbot. The facility was built in only a few months and housed around nine thousand soldiers. Over ninety thousand combat engineers trained there during the conflict, and it also housed German and Italian prisoners of war.

The war didn't erase the enormous accomplishments of the New Deal era, but after the attack on Pearl Harbor, the Forest Service had other priorities. In September 1942, Cleator wrote to a friend that the recreation business had been at "a very low ebb" since the start of the war and he had been reassigned to the fire control office.[372] The tone of the letter suggested that he wasn't thrilled with the reassignment.

After thirty-five years with the Forest Service, it must have seemed a good time to seek out other challenges. Cleator retired the following year at the age of sixty but continued important work with conservation and recreation. He became closely involved in the development of Forest Park in Portland. When dedicated in 1948, it was one of the largest urban forests in the United States.

In 1948, Cleator moved to Olympia, where he began working for Washington's Parks and Recreation Commission. His final project there had a surprising connection to his work on the Skyline Trail. In the

An informational pamphlet for the Frederick Cleator interpretive trails, Federation Forest State Park. *Courtesy of the Washington State Parks and Recreation Commission.*

years before his death, Cleator collaborated with the Washington State Federation of Women's Clubs to develop Federation Forest State Park along the White River, west of Tacoma. By coincidence, much of the land and funding for that project was donated by Catherine Montgomery, "Mother of the Pacific Crest Trail."

In her youth, Montgomery had been a suffragist, educational reformer and avid hiker. In 1926, she famously suggested the idea for the Pacific Crest Trail to Joseph Hazard, who helped popularize the notion. Although Cleator had expressed a similar sentiment during his Skyline survey of 1920, there is no evidence of him discussing it beyond his diary entry in a moment of inspiration atop Diamond Peak.

Montgomery died in 1957 in Bellingham, Washington at the age of ninety. She dedicated her estate to enlarging and improving Federation Forest State Park. Cleator died later that same year at the age of seventy-two, shortly after retiring from the Washington Parks and Recreation Commission.

Cleator and Montgomery, who first envisioned the Pacific Crest Trail, are memorialized at the park. The Catherine Montgomery Nature Interpretive Center hosts educational programs, and the adjacent interpretive trail is named in Cleator's honor.

The Skyline Trail was just one of Cleator's many accomplishments during a long career with the Forest Service. He played a central role in developing the early recreational areas across the Pacific Northwest and residential tracts in the national forests stretching from Mount Hood to Diamond Lake. During a stint in Washington State during the early 1920s, he developed the recreational plan for Lake Crescent and Lake Quinault in the Olympic National Forest.[373]

In the late 1920s, Cleator personally scouted sections of Washington's Cascade Crest Trail, stretching from the Canadian border to the Columbia River, and advocated for its development. Around the same time, he developed a comprehensive recreation plan for the Olympic Peninsula, which opened new recreation areas and preserved nearly half a million acres of wilderness in the Olympic National Forest and Enchanted Valley.

Although Cleator had suggested many place names during the Skyline survey that didn't survive, he's still credited with naming hundreds of other lakes, peaks and landmarks during his years with the Forest Service.[374] Today, he is remembered at several landmarks, including Mount Cleator in Washington's Glacier Peak Wilderness and the Cleator Bend Campground in the Willamette National Forest.

# 7

# PRESERVING AND PROTECTING THE TRAIL FOR FUTURE GENERATIONS

During the 1930s, there was a steady increase of users along the Skyline Trail. But it was far from what the boosters had promised in the early 1920s. Nevertheless, the creation of the Pacific Crest Trail System and YMCA Relays in the mid-1930s brought renewed interest in the trail. An unexpected boon of funding and labor from New Deal–era work programs helped the Forest Service significantly improve the route.

By the late 1930s, the original trail had been extended 35 miles from Mount Hood to the Columbia River and 115 miles from Crater Lake to the California border. Around 65 miles of its original path was rerouted to separate it from existing roadways. The Forest Service had enthusiastically embraced recreation as an important use of National Forest System lands and greatly expanded Oregon's recreational infrastructure, building thousands of campgrounds and hundreds of recreation facilities, including over 42,000 miles of foot trails.[375]

With the Skyline route fully established, the next challenge was protecting the wilderness lands surrounding the trail. Bob Marshall's brief tenure as the Forest Service's director of recreation and lands was pivotal in that fight. His work to strengthen the rules governing wilderness areas and founding the Wilderness Society laid the groundwork for the broader conservation movement and protection of public lands.

Clinton Clarke played a significant role in popularizing the route and advocating for its development. In 1935, he organized the Pacific Crest Trail

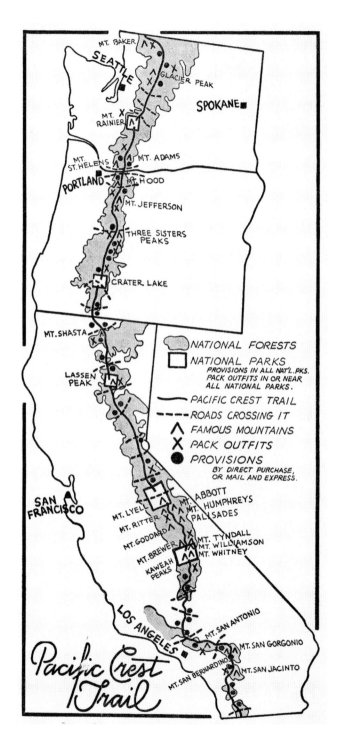

An early map of the
Pacific Crest Trail
appearing in *Sunset*
magazine, 1936.
*Courtesy of Sunset*
*magazine and the Pacific*
*Crest Trail Association.*

System Conference, which brought together an influential constituency of users able to plan, promote and protect the trail's route through Oregon and beyond. During his twenty-five years as conference president, Clarke recruited many prominent individuals to serve on the executive committee, including representatives from the YMCA, the Boy Scouts and the Sierra Club and the famous photographer Ansel Adams.[376]

By the early 1940s, the Skyline Trail was something very different from the initial plan proposed by the Forest Service two decades before. The concept for a scenic highway had been overly ambitious, reflecting the era's boundless enthusiasm for auto tourism. The new vision for the Skyline reflected important changes in how the Forest Service approached recreation and managed wilderness areas in the Cascades.

## A TRAIL FORGOTTEN

Despite the many accomplishments of the 1930s, much of the momentum for improving the trail was lost during the war years. After the publicity of the YMCA Relays, Clinton Clarke's influence waned, as did interest in the trail. With the start of World War II, the Forest Service quickly shifted to other priorities. The war created an unprecedented demand for wood products. The sudden industry turnaround was particularly notable in the Pacific Northwest. Oregon alone had provided almost 20 percent of the nation's lumber by the war's end.[377]

Even before the war, the Forest Service was reducing funding for recreation and trail work, particularly as New Deal–era work programs like the CCC were drawn down.[378] When the war began, thousands of Forest Service employees left for military service as CCC camps closed across the country. Recreational planning and trail development fell by the wayside. Consequently, little work was done on the Skyline route during the war, except as it served other Forest Service priorities.

Clinton Clarke continued to advocate for the Pacific Crest Trail during the war years despite few users. In 1945, he published the first comprehensive trail guide, *The Pacific Crest Trailway*. The book contained a brief history of the trail, covering the geography and natural environment. It included tips for backpacking and a suggested itinerary.

The guidebook had a detailed map of the entire route, including the locations of ranger stations, shelters, campgrounds and resupply points.

Clarke's book provided a sample gear list and recommendations for food to accommodate a two-week journey. He even included a proposed "program of awards" for trail accomplishments, such as covering certain distances in a single trip and summiting famous peaks along the route.

In the book's foreword, Clarke compared the trail to a necklace of gems, surrounded by a "permanent wilderness protected from all mechanization and commercialization."[379] He emphasized the trail's primitive nature, warning that it was "not a recreational project for the casual camper and hiker." Instead, it was something meant "for hardy adventurers who can enjoy the experience and benefits of a friendly struggle with Mother Nature."

Clarke saw the trail in moral terms. It was a defense against the evils of modernity and mechanization that had "created a soft, flabby civilization," leading to the "marked deterioration in the physical, mental and spiritual caliber of our youth."[380] He viewed the trail as a "serious educational program for building sturdy bodies, sound minds, and active, patriotic citizenship." If Clarke saw the trail as a test of stamina and character for "hardy adventurers," there were at least a few who were willing to take on that challenge.

## A Skyline First: Jack Meissner's Winter Ski Tour

During the 1930s, the Forest Service recognized the public's interest in wintertime recreation and began developing areas for snow sports adjacent to the Skyline route. Interest in skiing started in the late 1920s with the opening of the Summit Ski area at Government Camp in 1927, followed by Skibowl and Multorpor a few years later. The sport got an enormous boost with the opening of Timberline Lodge and Oregon's first chairlift, dubbed the Magic Mile, in November 1939.

The Forest Service was also developing winter recreation sites at other locations along the Skyline route. In the summer of 1939, CCC crews began construction of the Santiam Pass Ski Lodge just off US Highway 20. The Forest Service envisioned developing the area around Three Fingered Jack as a site for winter recreation.[381] However, due to its remote location, the area remained undeveloped. Instead, a small ski area opened on Hoodoo Butte in the late 1930s. During the area's first year of operation in 1941, over ten thousand people visited Santiam Pass for winter recreation. That same year, Willamette Pass Ski Area opened with a T-bar and several rope tows.

In 1948, a young ski instructor at Willamette Pass named Jack Meissner made an historic journey along the Skyline Trail. Meissner grew up on the Skyline. His family ran a small repair shop and marina at Shelter Cove, a popular trail stopover on the shores of Odell Lake. During World War II, Meissner served overseas as an aircraft mechanic, and when he returned from the war, he helped run his family's shop on the lake. During the winters, he ran trap lines in the surrounding forests and taught skiing at Willamette Pass.

During the winter of 1948, Meissner announced his plan for an epic 275-mile winter ski tour along the Skyline route from Mount Hood to Crater Lake. When the Forest Service heard about his plan, they warned against it due to the inherent dangers of traveling over such rugged terrain during wintertime.[382] The Mount Hood Ski Patrol took a similarly dim view of the adventure, calling it "foolhardy in the extreme."[383] Nevertheless, the Civil Air Patrol squadron based in Eugene agreed to help Meissner by dropping supplies along the route and occasionally checking on his progress from the air.

Meissner left Timberline Lodge in mid-February with fifty-five pounds of gear in an army surplus backpack, a compass and a Skyline Trail map. He estimated it would take him thirty days of skiing to reach Crater Lake. Meissner carried a tent and sleeping bag but planned to use the rustic three-sided Skyline shelters whenever possible. He planned two stopovers for rest and resupply at Santiam Pass and Odell Lake.[384]

He began the trip with a partner, a ski instructor at Timberline Lodge, but the man dropped out when they reached Mount Jefferson after suffering severe blisters. Before his departure, the pair had received their first parachute airdrop as they passed through Jefferson Park. The package contained a resupply of food and two carrier pigeons. Meissner released the birds into blizzard conditions with the message that he was continuing the trip alone. Amazingly, both birds flew through the storm and made it back to their cote in Eugene with Meissner's message.

It took twelve days for Meissner to complete the first one hundred miles to Santiam Pass. He tried his best to follow the Skyline Trail but found that many of the trail markers had been buried by the heavy snow that year.[385] Once he made it to Santiam Pass, Meissner took three days to rest and repair his equipment before setting out again.

After the stopover, Meissner encountered terrible weather as he made his way over McKenzie Pass. He missed the shelter near the Dee Wright Observatory and was forced to camp in the lava fields during the storm. He

Jack Meissner at Willamette Pass during his winter ski tour of the Skyline Trail, 1948. *Courtesy of Jane Meissner.*

later recalled that it was one of the most challenging moments of his entire trip.[386] The bad weather continued as he passed to the west of the Three Sisters. At one point, the storm became so severe that Meissner was forced to shelter in a snow cave.

After reaching South Sister in early March, Meissner received a second airdrop from the Civil Air Patrol. By the time he got to Waldo Lake, he decided to save time by crossing the frozen lake rather than skirting around the edge. A few days later, he made it to his parents' home on Odell Lake. He stayed there longer than planned due to inclement weather but made it to the Diamond Lake Lodge by early April, where he rested for a few days before starting the last leg of his journey. A week later, after thirty-three days on skis, Meissner ended the adventure at Crater Lake Lodge, becoming the first person to complete the Skyline Trail during wintertime.

Jack Meissner's accomplishment over the winter of 1948 would be one of several "firsts" on the trail in the coming decades. In 1952, Martin Papendick completed the first thru-hike of the Pacific Crest Trail, border to border. The year before, he had also been one of the first to complete the entire Appalachian Trail; however, his accomplishments were largely unknown at the time.[387]

In 1959, Don and June Mulford made the first verifiable equestrian thru-ride on the trail. The couple ran a cattle ranch at Castle Rock, Washington. Don had heard about the route while working with the CCC in Washington during the 1930s.[388] After that, he became captivated by the idea of riding it from end to end.

In April 1959, Don and June began their trip at the Mexican border with a string of five horses and a mule. They encountered challenges early on when one horse broke its leg and had to be euthanized. Another horse died of lockjaw a few weeks into the trip. They bought or traded horses along the way, and at Lake Tahoe, they added a mule named Handy Andy. Only two of the original horses made it the entire way to Canada.[389]

During the trip, they endured temperatures ranging from twenty to over one hundred degrees, along with fog, rain and snow. In the High Sierra, the couple had to detour around Mount Whitney, unable to navigate the deep snow near the pass. The Mulfords recorded their adventure using a 16-mm windup movie camera and fifty-four rolls of film. Don also kept a daily diary of the journey.

Don and June Mulford entering the Willamette National Forest along the Skyline Trail, August 1949. *Courtesy of June Mulford, Barney Scout Mann and Deems Burton.*

Don Mulford near Obsidian Cliffs in the Three Sisters Wilderness during their ride along the Pacific Crest Trail, August 1949. *Courtesy of June Mulford, Barney Scout Mann and Deems Burton.*

On August 11, the Mulfords passed through one of the most scenic spots on the Skyline Trail at Sisters Mirror Lake in the central Cascades. That day, Don wrote in his diary, "You may think one would get tired of so much scenery, day after day, but June and I will never get tired of the outdoors, the scenery, or the clean mountain air out here."[390] After five months and a week, they reached the Canadian border at the end of September. Despite the hardships, Don later called it the "adventure of a lifetime."[391]

## Growing Government Involvement in Outdoor Recreation

The postwar decades brought an enormous increase in outdoor recreation as Americans enjoyed more leisure time and mobility. Much of this activity occurred on public lands, especially the national forests. In the Pacific Northwest, forest visits jumped from 3.8 million to 5.2 million between 1952 and 1955.[392] Faced with a surge of new users, the agency began a major effort to expand recreational facilities such as campgrounds, trails and ski areas.

One reflection of this change was the passage of the Multiple Use-Sustained Yield Act of 1960. The act is considered one of the first environmental protection laws because it mandated the maintenance of renewable resources in the national forests without impairing land productivity. Also, for the first time, the law elevated recreation to an equal status among the other uses.[393] With the growing importance of recreation, the agency realized it needed better information to develop policy and plan for future needs.

In 1958, Congress created the Outdoor Recreation Resources Review Commission to study the issue. The commission was chaired by the noted philanthropist and conservationist Laurance Rockefeller. Congress tasked the commission with assessing the country's recreational needs and resources and making recommendations on future policies and programs. The study resulted in the *Outdoor Recreation for America* report, submitted to President Kennedy in January 1962.

Among the report's key findings was that 90 percent of Americans participated in some form of outdoor recreation each year.[394] The commission found that basic outdoor activities like walking, swimming, and picnicking were the most popular. However, many recreational areas weren't satisfying user needs due to their remote location, lack of infrastructure or restrictive land designations.[395]

One of the report's key recommendations was improving the preservation of scenic areas, natural wonders and primitive areas for recreation. To achieve this, the commission recommended an updated system for classifying recreational lands with added protections for "undisturbed roadless areas characterized by natural, wild conditions, including wilderness areas."

At the same time, Secretary of the Interior Stewart Udall requested that the Bureau of Outdoor Recreation examine the status of the nation's trails, with the ambitious goal of building 100,000 miles of new trails in the national forests and parks.[396] The study resulted in the *Trails for America* report of 1965. Among the report's recommendations was the creation of a national trail system, including two major long-distance routes to be designated as national scenic trails. Those trails were defined as offering continuous, extended outdoor recreation routes within protected corridors.[397]

The study became the basis for the National Trails System Act of 1968, which designated the Appalachian Trail and the Pacific Crest Trail as the first two national scenic trails. The act reinforced wilderness protections along the trail by allowing only campsites, shelters and related facilities while prohibiting motorized vehicles. The law also financed and facilitated the acquisition of lands to improve trail corridors and create a network of feeder routes.

Hikers entering the Skyline Trail near Breitenbush campground, 1965. *Photo by Bob Unruh. U.S. Forest Service.*

The growing political momentum to establish protected recreation areas led to the passage of the landmark Wilderness Act of 1964, considered one of the most important pieces of conservation legislation in American history. Bob Marshall's important work in the late 1930s set the stage for that achievement, spearheaded by the later work of Howard Zahniser at the Wilderness Society. The law immediately affected the Skyline Trail by

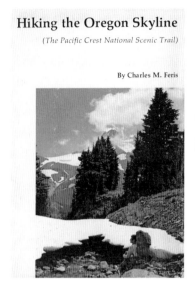

# Hiking the Oregon Skyline

*(The Pacific Crest National Scenic Trail)*

By Charles M. Feris

*Left*: Cover of an Oregon Skyline Trail guidebook by Charles Feris, 1973. *Oregon Historical Society.*

*Above*: One of the few remaining Skyline Trail signs after the establishment of the Pacific Crest Trail, 1971. *U.S. Forest Service.*

buttressing existing protections covering tens of thousands of acres along the route.

The Wilderness Act protected and preserved designated wildernesses in their natural condition without permanent improvements or habitation. The act prohibited commercial enterprise and permanent roads within the designated areas. The new law immediately redesignated several large sections along the Skyline Trail, including the Mount Hood, Three Sisters, Mount Washington, and Diamond Peak Wildernesses. The Mount Jefferson Wilderness was added to the list four years later.

After decades of debate about managing and protecting the land surrounding the Skyline Trail, the Wilderness Act ensured that most of the route would be preserved in its natural state, unthreatened by development or the incursion of mechanized vehicles. The Wilderness Act created an important legal precedent for later additions along the route. In 1984, Congress passed the Oregon Wilderness Act, adding nearly one million acres of federal land to the National Wilderness Preservation System. This legislation doubled the state's federally protected wilderness areas, adding Waldo Lakes, Mount Thielsen, Sky Lakes and the Hatfield Wildernesses to the protected areas along the old Skyline route.

## CONCLUSION

President Lyndon Johnson's signing of the National Trails Systems Act in 1968 was an enormous victory for conservation and recreation groups advocating for "the forgotten outdoorsmen" who wanted to walk, hike and ride in spaces free of mechanized activity.[398] The law provided new authorities and funding to improve public access, acquire lands, protect rights of way and preserve wilderness corridors along America's scenic trails. The legislation also designated the Pacific Crest Trail as one of the first two national scenic trails.

While the designation was good for the Pacific Crest Trail, it also meant that the legacy of the Skyline Trail was gradually forgotten. Growing interest in hiking during the late 1960s and early 1970s spurred the publication of updated trail maps and guidebooks. In 1973, Thomas Winnett, founder of Wilderness Press, published volume one of the first Pacific Crest Trail guidebook covering California.[399] The Oregon and Washington volumes came the following year.

By the time the Pacific Crest Trail was declared officially "completed" in 1993, much of the origin story of the Oregon section had slipped from common knowledge. The iconic white Pacific Crest Trail diamonds gradually replaced the remaining Skyline Trail signs left over from the 1920s. While forgotten, Oregon's Skyline Trail was the foundation upon which the Pacific Crest Trail was built. It was the Forest Service's first long-distance recreational trail and became a model for subsequent trail development across the country.

Over the years, the Pacific Crest Trail has veered somewhat from the Skyline route, but occasionally one can catch glimpses of Cleator's original path. Sometimes it appears as an overgrown forest road or an abandoned footpath running parallel to the current Pacific Crest Trail. Today, few of the old Waldo and Bingham trees exist outside of museums. But a handful of Cleator's original Skyline blazes can still be spotted, recognizable as distinctive vertical slashes carved in the trees.

Occasionally, one will find an old rusting nail hammered into a tree that once held a Skyline Trail sign. At a few sites are the rotting remains of the trail shelters built by the CCC crews during the 1930s. Beyond those fading clues, what is most indelible is Cleator's meticulously placed route, designed to highlight "the ruggedness of the mountains, the alpine meadows, the high mesas and volcanic formations as intimately as possible."[400] In blazing the Skyline Trail, Cleator and those who went before him created a lasting gift to the citizens of Oregon.

# NOTES

## Introduction

1. "Proposed Skyline Road Held Practical," *Morning Oregonian*, 3.

## 1. A Natural and Cultural History of the Oregon Cascades

2. Miller, *Roadside Geology*, 111–16.
3. Stuart et al., *Atlas of Oregon*, 167.
4. Orr and Orr, *Oregon Geology*, 155–85.
5. Stuart et al., *Atlas of Oregon*, 135.
6. Sherrod, "Cascade Mountain Range."
7. Orr and Orr, *Oregon Geology*, 177.
8. Sherrod, "Cascade Mountain Range."
9. Pater, *Ecoregions of Western Washington*.
10. Ibid.
11. Oregon Department of Fish and Wildlife, *Oregon Conservation Strategy*.
12. Toedtemeier and Laursen, *Wild Beauty*, 9.
13. W. Clark, *Journals of the Lewis and Clark Expedition*, April 16, 1806.
14. Lewis, "Outside the Ethnographic Box."
15. Stuart et al., *Atlas of Oregon*, 10.
16. Zenk, "Molalla Peoples."
17. Lewis, "Ethnographic Molalla Homelands."
18. Oregon Trails Coordinating Council, *Oregon Historic Trails Report* [hereafter *Trails Report*], 81.

19. Ibid., 77.
20. Sturtevant and Walker, *Handbook of North American Indians*, 443.
21. Jenkins, Aikens and Connolly, *Oregon Archaeology*, 189.
22. Farmer and Holmes, *Historical Atlas of Early Oregon*, 9–10.
23. Williams, "Expeditions, Explorations, and Journeys," 11.
24. Brogan, *East of the Cascades*, 28–29.
25. Walker, "Cartography of Oregon."
26. Wilkes, "Report on the Territory," 272.
27. Winch, *Biography of a Place*, 39.
28. *Trails Report*, 183.
29. Winch, *Biography of a Place*, 40.
30. Sawyer, "Abbot Railroad Surveys," 2–3.
31. *Reports of Explorations and Surveys*, vol. 6, 77–79; Sawyer, "Abbot Railroad Surveys," 17.
32. Beckham, *Oregon Central Military Wagon Road*, 13.
33. Young, "Mount Hood."
34. Abbot, *Report of Lieut. Henry L. Abbot*, 102.
35. Abbot and Williamson, *Report of the Corps of Topographical Engineers*, 30.
36. Atwood, *Chaining Oregon*, 209.
37. Stuart et al., *Atlas of Oregon*, 22.
38. Minto, "Minto Pass," 242.
39. Minto, "Youth to Age," 157.
40. Minor and Pecor, *Cultural Resource Overview*, 16.
41. Winch, *Biography of a Place*, 42.
42. Minor and Pecor, *Cultural Resource Overview*, 155.
43. *Trails Report*, 233.
44. Williams, "McKenzie Pass."
45. Winch, *Biography of a Place*, 55.
46. Sawyer, "Beginnings of McKenzie Highway," 264.
47. Williams, "Expeditions, Explorations, and Journeys," 31.
48. Beckham, *Oregon Central Military Wagon Road*, 20.
49. Merriam, "First Oregon Cavalry," 91.
50. Beckham, *Oregon Central Military Wagon Road*, 46.
51. Minto, "Youth to Age," 152.
52. Minor and Pecor, *Cultural Resource Overview*, 155.
53. Minto, "Youth to Age," 157.
54. Maxwell, "Waldo, Salem Jurist," 4.

## 2. Blazing the Path: Judge Waldo
## and the Cascade Range Forest Reserve

55. Williams, "Expeditions, Explorations, and Journeys," 27.
56. Mark, "On an Old Road."
57. Rogue River–Siskiyou National Forest, "Rogue River," II-1.
58. Snead, *Judge John B. Waldo*, 10.
59. Knight, "Judge John B. Waldo," 39.
60. Lalande, "Wilderness Journey with Judge John B. Waldo," 120.
61. Snead, *Judge John B. Waldo*, 11.
62. Ibid., 7.
63. Waldo, Journals and Letters, August 7, 1884, 6.
64. Thomas, *Oregon High*, 85.
65. Hatton, *High Country*, 17.
66. Snead, *Judge John B. Waldo*, 26.
67. Lalande, "John B. Waldo."
68. Snead, *Judge John B. Waldo*, 31–35.
69. Lalande, "Wilderness Journey," 120.
70. Ibid., 124.
71. Snead, *Judge John B. Waldo*, 45.
72. Lalande, "Wilderness Journey," 140.
73. Williams and Mark, *Establishing and Defending the Cascade Range*, 23–24.
74. Atwood et al. "Utility and Service Combined with Beauty," 6.
75. Waldo, Journals and Letters, September 4, 1890, 44.
76. Corning, "Dee Wright," 274–75.
77. Mansayon, "Henry Yelkus."
78. Stivers, "Saga of the Skyline Trail," 5.
79. Mark, "William Gladstone Steel."
80. Williams, *U.S. Forest Service*, 37.
81. Snead, *Judge John B. Waldo*, 7–10.
82. Williams, "John B. Waldo and William Steel," 314.
83. Williams and Mark, *Establishing and Defending the Cascade Range*, 55.
84. Snead, *Judge John B. Waldo*, 73.
85. Ibid., 75–58.
86. Williams and Mark, *Establishing and Defending the Cascade Range*, 116–17.
87. Rakestraw, "Sheep Grazing in the Cascade Range," 372.
88. Williams and Mark, *Establishing and Defending the Cascade Range*," 212.
89. Ibid., 271–76.
90. Williams, "John B. Waldo and William G. Steel," 328.
91. Unrau, *Administrative History*, 62.
92. Pinchot, *Breaking New Ground*, 101–2.

93. Mark, "William Gladstone Steel."

94. Waldo, Journals and Letters, September 16, 1896, 11.

95. Williams, *U.S. Forest Service*, 41.

96. Rakestraw, "Sheep Grazing in the Cascade Range," 376–77.

97. Williams and Mark, *Establishing and Defending the Cascade Range*, 616–17.

98. Waldo, Journals and Letters, August 16, 1906, 104.

99. "Judge Waldo Is Dead," *Capital Journal*, 1.

100. Waldo, Journals and Letters, 107.

101. Knight, "Judge John B. Waldo," 38.

102. Joslin, "Cyrus Bingham."

103. Atwood et al., "Utility and Service Combined with Beauty," 65.

104. Cox, *Blazes on the Skyline*, 5.

105. Coady, *Cyrus James Bingham*, chapter 6.

106. Ibid., chapter 4.

107. Cox, *Blazes on the Skyline*, 54.

108. Newman, "Book Examines Life," 2G.

109. Krechel, "Forest Service and Cy J. Bingham," 166.

110. Cox, *Blazes on the Skyline*, 55.

111. Williams, "John B. Waldo and William G. Steel," 329.

112. Williams, *U.S. Forest Service*, 49.

113. Rakestraw and Rakestraw, *History of the Willamette*, 60–61.

114. Woolley, *Off to Mt. Hood*, 11.

115. *Trails Report*, 235.

116. Williams, "Willamette Pass."

117. Aurand and Carpenter, *First Century of Oregon State Parks*, 12.

118. Unrau, *Administrative History*, 553.

119. Toedtememeier and Laursen, *Wild Beauty*, 198.

120. Oregon Department of Transportation, "Historic Columbia River Highway."

121. Maher, *Nature's New Deal*, 139

122. Toedtememeier and Laursen, *Wild Beauty*, 199.

123. "Park Promised by Forester Graves," *Sunday Oregonian*, 14.

124. Hale, "Now 100 Years Old."

125. Peterson del Mar, *Oregon's Promise*, 162.

126. Sutter, *Driven Wild*, 62.

127. Kelly, "Oregon Roads Famous," 7.

128. Aurand and Carpenter, *First Century of Oregon State Parks*, 15–16.

129. "Proposed Skyline Road," *Morning Oregonian*, 3.

130. Ibid.

131. Ibid.

132. Ibid.

## 3. Changes on the Land: The Forest Service, Conservation and Outdoor Recreation

133. Chamberlin, *On the Trail*, xiii.
134. Brock and Grauer, "Mazamas."
135. Weiselberg, "He All but Made the Mountains," 56.
136. Ibid., 64.
137. Riddell, "Three Sisters Outing," 10–11.
138. Henthorne, "Three Sisters Outing, 1916," 7–23.
139. "Mazamas Return with Stories," *Oregon Daily Journal*.
140. "Mazamas to Shift Summer Settings," *Sunday Oregonian*.
141. Parker, "Twenty-Ninth Annual Mazama Outing," 7–20.
142. Williams, *U.S. Forest Service*, 94.
143. Tweed, "History of Outdoor Recreation Development," 1.
144. Gildor, "Location, Location, Location," 996.
145. Young, *Heading Out*, 134.
146. Nye, "Camping in the National Forests."
147. Tweed, "Recreation Site Planning and Improvements," 2.
148. Building Oregon, "Cabin, Camp Sherman Recreational Residences," 3.
149. Stark, "Mapping of Our National Forests," 27.
150. Steen, *U.S. Forest Service*, 158.
151. Waugh, "Recreational Uses," 3–4.
152. Ibid., 7–9.
153. Waugh, "Landscape Engineering."
154. Barker, "Through Oregon on High," 61.
155. Sutter, "Blank Spot on the Map," 187.
156. Maher, *Nature's New Deal*, 165.
157. Leopold, "Wilderness and Its Place," 719.
158. Ibid.
159. Oregon Department of Transportation, "History of State Highways in Oregon," 14.
160. Sutter, "Blank Spot on the Map," 199.
161. Young, *Heading Out*, 137.
162. Nye, "Camping in the National Forests."
163. Caldbick, "Frederick William Cleator."
164. Cleator, "Recreation Objectives," 467–75.
165. U.S. Forest Service, "Diamond Lake Recreational Residence Tract," 24.
166. Tweed, *History of Outdoor Recreation Development*, 13.
167. Donovan and Tonsfeldt. "Mt. Hood National Forest," 6.
168. Williams, *U.S. Forest Service*, 95.
169. Vora, "History of the Recreation Residence Program," 13.

170. Williams, *U.S. Forest Service*, 99.

171. Oregon State Highway Commission, "Tentative Plan, 1916."

172. Barker, "Oregon Skyline Trail," 52.

173. Harry, "Close Rough View of Peak," 1.

174. "Plans Progress to Complete Trails," *Oregon Daily Journal*, 15.

175. "Jefferson Park to Have Trails," *Oregon Daily Journal*, 4.

176. Anderson, *We Had an Objective in Mind*, 54.

177. White, *Story of Lige Coalman*, 54.

178. Grauer, *Mount Hood*, 133.

179. "Kiser Photo Company."

180. "Highway Plea Is Made," *Morning Oregonian*.

181. "Will Use Pictures as Road Propaganda," *Bend Bulletin*.

182. "Oregon Country Realizes Dream," *Oregon Daily Journal*.

## 4. Mapping the Skyline: Frederick Cleator's 1920 Reconnaissance

183. Barker, "Through Oregon on High," 51.

184. Rakestraw and Rakestraw, *History of the Willamette*, 71.

185. Cleator, "Skyline Diaries," 1–2.

186. Cleator, "Report of Preliminary Investigation," 1.

187. Rakestraw and Rakestraw, *History of the Willamette*, 65.

188. Gray, "Radio for the Fireline," 11–12; Deacon, "Birds Come to the Rescue."

189. Barker, "Oregon Skyline Trail," 55.

190. Tweed, *History of Outdoor Recreation Development*, 19.

191. McClelland, *Presenting Nature*, chapter 7.

192. Ibid.

193. Barker, "Through Oregon on High," 64.

194. Throop, "Recreation Development," 32.

195. Cleator, "Skyline Diaries," 1.

196. U.S. Forest Service, "Diamond Lake Recreational Residence Tract," 33–35.

197. Cleator, "Skyline Diaries," 2.

198. Williams, *U.S. Forest Service*, 99.

199. Cleator, "Skyline Diaries," 4.

200. Ibid., 6.

201. Cleator, "Tales of the Oregon Skyline," 4.

202. Cleator, "Skyline Diaries," 8.

203. Cleator, "Tales of the Oregon Skyline," 7.

204. Cleator, "Skyline Diaries," 9–10.

205. Cleator, "Tales of the Oregon Skyline," 10.

206. Cleator, "Skyline Diaries," 12–13.

207. Ibid., 16–18.

208. Eldridge, *James Oliver Curwood.*

209. Cleator, "Skyline Diaries," 21–22.

210. Ibid., 25–28.

211. Cermak, "Pioneering Aerial Forest Fire Control," 292.

212. Lalande, "Aerial Forest-Fire Patrol Program in Oregon."

213. Cleator, "Skyline Diaries," 30–31.

214. McArthur, *Oregon Geographic Names*, 169.

215. Cleator, "Skyline Diaries," 37–39.

216. Ibid., 38.

217. Ibid., 42–44.

218. Ibid., 44-47.

219. Cleator, "Report of Preliminary Investigation Oregon Skyline Route," 7.

220. Cleator, "Skyline Diaries," 48–49.

221. Vora, "History of the Recreation Residence Program," 13.

222. Cleator, "Report of Preliminary Investigation Oregon Skyline Route," 2.

223. Ibid., 3.

224. Williams, *U.S. Forest Service*, 100.

225. Stark, "Mapping of Our National Forests," 93.

226. Stark, "Names, Boundaries, and Maps," 429–30.

227. Oregon Tourist and Information Bureau, "Oregon Skyline Trail Map."

228. "Some Wonder Scenes Proposed," *Oregon Sunday Journal*, 3.

229. MacKaye, "Appalachian Trail," 325–30.

## 5. Selling the Skyline: Outdoor Recreation in the Age of Auto Tourism

230. Cleator, "Tale of the Oregon Skyline," 1.

231. Tweed, *History of Outdoor Recreational Development*, 5.

232. Barker, "Oregon Skyline Trail," 55.

233. Mitchell, "Ambivalent Landscapes," 34–40.

234. "Will Use Pictures as Road Propaganda," *Bend Bulletin*, 1.

235. "Creation of a Great Public Park," *Bend Bulletin*, 1.

236. "Proposed Skyline Road through Cascades," *Morning Oregonian*, 3.

237. "Road Would Tap Scenic Wonderland," *Morning Oregonian*, 11.

238. "$1,00,000 Will Build Highway," *Oregon Sunday Journal*, 2.

239. "Skyline Trail Would Open Scenic Wonders," *Sunday Oregonian*, 1.

240. Kelly, "Oregon Roads Famous," 7.

241. Hoyt, "Good Roads Movement in Oregon," 62.

242. Cain, "LaGrande-Wallowa Lake Highway."

243. Atwood et al., "Utility and Service Combined with Beauty," 22.

244. "Some Wonder Scenes Proposed."

245. "Oregon Skyline Trail Rich in Rare Scenery," *Sunday Oregonian*.

246. "Some Scenic Highways of the Future," *Sunday Oregonian*.

247. Clinton, "Pictorial Maps of Fred A. Routledge," 45.

248. Ibid., 62–63.

249. "Magazine Writer Will Take Hike over the Cascades," *Morning Register*, 8.

250. Eaton, "On the Skyline Trail," B43.

251. Ibid.

252. Eaton, *Skyline Camps*, 266.

253. Ibid.,168.

254. Eaton, *Boy Scouts at Crater Lake*, 239.

255. "Skyline Trail," *Oregon Daily Journal*, 10.

256. Author correspondence with Barney Scout Mann, September 13, 2023.

257. Mann, "Was This Swedish Immigrant the First."

258. Barker, "Through Oregon on High," 100.

259. "Trip on the Skyline Evokes Interest," *Sunday Oregonian*, 6.

260. "Skyline Party Planned," *Sunday Oregonian*, 14.

261. Cleator, "History of the Oregon Skyline," 1.

262. Coady, *Cyrus James Bingham*, chapter "Government Work."

263. "Knowles Celebrate Golden Wedding," *Eugene Guard*, 32.

264. Knowles, *Honeymoon on Horseback*, 17.

265. Ibid., 54.

266. Ibid., 102.

267. "Feminine Trend on Skyline Trail Seen," *Bend Bulletin*, 8.

268. "Girl Completes 2000-Mile Hike to Crater Lake," *Medford Mail Tribune*, 1.

269. MacKaye, "Appalachian Trail," 325–30.

270. D'Anieri, *Appalachian Trail*, 86–92.

271. MacKaye, "Appalachian Trail," 3.

272. Sutter, *Driven Wild*, 159.

273. Anderson, "Benton MacKaye and the Path to the First AT Conference," 17–21.

274. Sutter, *Driven Wild*, 159.

275. Chamberlin, *On the Trail*, 132.

276. Anderson, *Benton MacKaye*, 230.

277. King, "Era of Trail Protection," 12.

278. Holstine and Bruce, "Historical Overview."

279. Mann, "No, It's Montgomery," 9–11.

280. "New Bend Group Will Be Named," *Bend Bulletin*, 1.

281. Colburn, "Mary Carolyn Davies."

282. "Skyline Trail," *Eastern Clackamas News*, 2.

283. "Glimpses of Oregon Country," *Morning Oregonian*, 11.

284. "New Skyline Trail Map," *Evening Herald*, 5.

285. "Glimpses of Oregon Country," *Morning Oregonian*, 11.
286. Barker, "Oregon Skyline Trail," 69.

## 6. Reinventing the Skyline: The New Deal and the Pacific Crest Trail

287. Steen, *U.S. Forest Service*, 156.
288. Ibid., 199–202.
289. Marshall, "Problem of the Wilderness," 142.
290. Marshall, "Forest for Recreation," 465.
291. Rakestraw and Rakestraw, *History of the Willamette*, 139.
292. Williams, "Civilian Conservation Corps," 8.
293. Williams, *U.S. Forest Service*, 116–17.
294. Otis et al., "Forest Service and the Civilian Conservation Corps," 11.
295. Williams, "Civilian Conservation Corps," 6.
296. Atwood et al., "Utility and Service Combined with Beauty," 28.
297. Rakestraw and Rakestraw, *History of the Willamette*, 113.
298. Otis et al., "Forest Service and The Civilian Conservation Corps," 46.
299. Tweed, *History of Outdoor Recreation Development*, 16.
300. Rakestraw and Rakestraw, *History of the Willamette*, 108.
301. Tweed, *History of Outdoor Recreation Development*, 22.
302. Rakestraw and Rakestraw, *History of the Willamette*, 70.
303. Barker, "Oregon on High," 106.
304. "New Skyline Trail Being Built," *Eugene Guard*, 2.
305. Williams, *U.S. Forest Service*, 145.
306. Rakestraw and Rakestraw, *History of the Willamette*, 108.
307. Barker, "Oregon on High," 105.
308. "Skyline Trail Completion Is Due," *Oregon Statesman*, 3.
309. Cleator, "Instructions for Extensive Examination," 1.
310. Cleator, "Report of Preliminary Investigation," 7.
311. "New Skyline Trail Being Built," *Eugene Guard*, 2.
312. "On the Skyline," *Bend Bulletin*.
313. "New Skyline Trail Being Built."
314. Williams, *U.S. Forest Service*, 155; "Dee Wright Dies Here on Tuesday," *Eugene Guard*.
315. Krechel, "Forest Service and Cy J. Bingham," 169.
316. "Dee Wright," *Bend Bulletin*, 4.
317. Barker, "Oregon on High," 105–6.
318. "Skyline Trail Surveyed," *Morning Oregonian*, 6.
319. Royer, "Skyline Trail," 17.

320. Ibid., 1.
321. "Skyline Trail Topic," *Eugene Guard*, 8
322. Royer, "Skyline Trail," 14.
323. Ibid., 29.
324. Tweed, *History of Outdoor Recreation Development*, 25.
325. Glover, *Wilderness Original*, 253.
326. Glover, "Romance, Recreation, and Wilderness," 36.
327. Maher, *Nature's New Deal*, 150.
328. Fox, "We Want No Straddlers," 8.
329. Marshall, "Forest for Recreation," 472.
330. Ibid., 474.
331. Maher, *Nature's New Deal*, 173.
332. Ibid., 162.
333. Steen, *U.S. Forest Service*, 211.
334. Williams, *U.S. Forest Service*, 145; Roth, "National Forests," 125.
335. Stark, "Names, Boundaries, and Maps," 21.
336. Williams, *U.S. Forest Service*, 140.
337. Rakestraw and Rakestraw, *History of the Willamette*, 143.
338. "Anglers to Meet at Silverton," *Oregon Statesman*, 6.
339. Williams, *U.S. Forest Service*, 140.
340. Glover, *Wilderness Original*, 253.
341. Joslin, *Three Sisters Wilderness*, 22.
342. Cleator, Letter to Charles Paul Keyser, 2.
343. Ibid.
344. Ibid.
345. Rakestraw and Rakestraw, *History of the Willamette*, 146.
346. Ibid., 107.
347. Cleator, "Recollections of Bob Marshall," 3.
348. Ibid.
349. Williams, *U.S. Forest Service*, 147.
350. Glover, *Wilderness Original*, 263.
351. Joslin, *Three Sisters Wilderness*, 22–23.
352. Caldbick, "Frederick William Cleator."
353. Glover, *Wilderness Original*, 267–70.
354. Cleator, "Recollections of Bob Marshall," 12.
355. Marshall, Letter to Frederick Cleator, October 2, 1939.
356. Pacific Crest Trail Association, "Founders of the Pacific Crest Trail."
357. Author correspondence with Barney Scout Mann, September 13, 2023.
358. Chamberlin, "On the Trail," 134–35.
359. Rogers, *PCT Relays*, 3.

360. Mann, "Pacific Crest Trail Blazer."

361. "Eight Groups to Trek," *Evening Herald*, 6.

362. Rogers, *PCT Relays*, 57.

363. "Skyline Trail Marked by New Signs," *Bonneville Dam Chronicle*, 12.

364. Cleator, Letter to Una Davies, Trails Club of Oregon, February 16, 1956.

365. Ibid.

366. Rakestraw and Rakestraw, *History of the Willamette*, 108.

367. Barker, "Oregon on High," 92.

368. "Skyline Trail Topic for Club Meeting," *Eugene Guard*, 8.

369. Cleator, "Skyline Diaries," 9–10.

370. "Beauty of Cascade Skyline Trail Shown," *Eugene Guard*, 8.

371. Williams, *U.S. Forest Service*, 128.

372. Cleator, Letter to A.D. Taylor, September 23, 1942.

373. Evans, "Historic Resource Study," chapter 4.

374. Caldbick, "Frederick William Cleator."

## *7. Preserving and Protecting the Trail for Future Generations*

375. Tweed, *History of Outdoor Recreation Development*, 26; Williams, *U.S. Forest Service*, 118–19.

376. Pacific Crest Trail Association, "Founders of the Pacific Crest Trail."

377. Atwood et al., "Utility and Service Combined with Beauty," 34.

378. Cleator, "Status and Use of the Pacific Crest Trail," 1.

379. Clark, *Pacific Crest Trailway*, 11.

380. Ibid., 21.

381. Lindberg, "Santiam Pass Ski Lodge."

382. "Meissner Looks for Partner," *Herald and News*, 8.

383. Hamlin, "Greatest Ski Adventure."

384. "Two Men Start Ski Trip," *Bend Bulletin*, 8.

385. Watters, "Jack Meissner."

386. Hamlin, "Greatest Ski Adventure."

387. Howell, "Exploring the History."

388. Mann, "Giving Trail History Its Due," 13.

389. Author correspondence with Barney Mann, September 13, 2023.

390. Mann, "Across the Snowy Crest."

391. Fuller, "Couple Fulfill Dream," 4.

392. Williams, *U.S. Forest Service*, 188.

393. Steen, *U.S. Forest Service*, 298–99.

394. Dilsaver, *America's National Park System*, chapter 5.

395. Outdoor Recreation Resources Review Commission, *Outdoor Recreation for America*.

396. U.S. Department of the Interior, *Trails for America*.

397. U.S. Congress, National Trails System Act, 1968.

398. President Lyndon Johnson, "Special Message to Congress," February 8, 1965.

399. Mann, "Making of the First Pacific Crest Trail Guidebook."

400. Barker, "Oregon on High," 64.

# BIBLIOGRAPHY

*Books and Monographs*

Anderson, Larry. *Benton MacKaye: Conservationist, Planner and Creator of the Appalachian Trail.* Baltimore, MD: Johns Hopkins University Press, 2002.

———. "Benton MacKaye and the Path to the First AT Conference." In *Trail Years: A History of the Appalachian Trail Conference*, 17–22. Harpers Ferry, WV: Appalachian Trail Conference, 2000.

Anderson, Rolf, ed. *We Had an Objective in Mind: The U.S. Forest Service in the Pacific Northwest, 1905 to 2005.* Portland, OR: Pacific Northwest Forest Association, 2005.

Atwood, Kay. *Chaining Oregon: Surveying the Public Lands of the Pacific Northwest, 1851–1855.* Blacksburg, VA: McDonald & Woodward Publishing Company, 2008.

Aurand, Marin, and Marc Carpenter. *The First Century of Oregon State Parks.* Salem: Oregon Parks and Recreation Department, 2022.

Brogan, Phil. *East of the Cascades.* Portland, OR: Binfords & Mort Publishers, 1964.

Chamberlin, Silas. *On the Trail: A History of American Hiking.* New Haven, CT: Yale University Press, 2016.

Clark, Clinton. *The Pacific Crest Trailway.* Pasadena, CA: Pacific Crest Trail System Conference, 1945.

Coady, Steven. *Cyrus James Bingham from Michigan Westward.* 1st ed. United States: CreateSpace Independent Publishing, 2014.

Cohen, Michael. *A History of the Sierra Club: 1892–1970.* San Francisco, CA: Sierra Club Books, 1988.

Corning, Howard McKinley, ed. "Dee Wright." In *Dictionary of Oregon History*, 274–75. Portland, OR: Binford & Mort Publishing, 1956.

Cox, Robert Hall. *Blazes on the Skyline*. United States: Pacific House Books, 1988.

Cox, Thomas R. *The Park Builders: A History of State Parks in the Pacific Northwest*. Seattle: University of Washington Press, 1988.

D'Anieri, Philip. *The Appalachian Trail: A Biography*. Boston: Mariner Books, 2021.

Dilsaver, Lary, ed. *America's National Park System: The Critical Documents*. Lanham, MD: Rowman & Littlefield Publishers, 1994.

Eaton, Walter Prichard. *Boy Scouts at Crater Lake*. Boston, MA: W.A. Wilde Company, 1922.

————. *Skyline Camps: A Note Book of a Wanderer in Our Northwest Mountains*. Boston, MA: W.A. Wilde Company, 1922.

Eldridge, Judith A. *James Oliver Curwood: God's Country and the Man*. Bowling Green, OH: Bowling Green State University Press, 1993.

Farmer, Judith, and Kenneth Holmes. *An Historical Atlas of Early Oregon*. Portland, OR: Historical Cartographic Publications, 1973.

Feris, Charles. *Hiking the Oregon Skyline Trail*. Beaverton, OR: Touchstone Press, 1973.

Glover, James. *A Wilderness Original: The Life of Bob Marshall*. Seattle, WA: The Mountaineers, 1986.

Grauer, Jack. *Mount Hood: A Complete History*. 8th ed. Vancouver, WA: Jack Grauer, 2010.

Hatton, Raymond. *High Country of Central Oregon*. Portland, OR: Binford & Mort Publishing, 1980.

Hughes, Rees, and Corey Lee Lewis, eds. *The Pacific Crest Trail Reader: Oregon and Washington*. Seattle, WA: The Mountaineers, 2011.

Jenkins, Dennis, Melvin Aikens and Thomas Connolly. *Oregon Archaeology*. Corvallis: Oregon State University Press, 2011.

Joslin, Les. *Three Sisters Wilderness: A History*. Charleston, SC: The History Press, 2021.

King, Brian. "The Era of Trail Protection." In *Trail Years: A History of the Appalachian Trail Conference*, 12–16. Harpers Ferry, WV: Appalachian Trail Conference, 2000.

Knight, Steve. "Judge John B. Waldo: Defender of the High Cascades." In *Little Known Tails from Oregon History*, vol. 2: 38–44. Bend, OR: Sun Publishing, 1991.

Knowles, Margie Young. *Honeymoon on Horseback*. New York: Carlton Press, 1970.

Lowe, Beverly Elizabeth. *John Minto: Man of Courage, 1822–1915*. Salem, OR: Kingston Price and Company, 1980.

Maher, Neil. *Nature's New Deal*. New York: Oxford University Press, 2008.

McArthur, Lewis A. *Oregon Geographic Names*. 5th ed. Portland: Oregon Historical Society, 1982.

McClelland, Linda. *Presenting Nature: The Historic Landscape Design of the National Park Service: 1916 to 1942*. Washington, D.C.: National Park Service, 1993.

Miller, Marli. *Roadside Geology of Oregon*. 2nd ed. Missoula, MT: Mountain Press Publishing Company, 2014.

Nash, Roderick Frazier. *Wilderness and the American Mind*. New Haven, CT: Yale University Press, 2001.

Orr, Elizabeth, and William Orr. *Oregon Geology*. 6th ed. Corvallis: Oregon State University Press, 2012.

Peterson del Mar, David. *Oregon's Promise: An Interpretive History*. Corvallis: Oregon State University Press, 2003.

Pinchot, Gifford. *Breaking New Ground*. New York: Harcourt, Brace and Company, 1947.

Rogers, Warren. *The PCT Relays*. Santa Ana, CA: Warren Rogers, 1968.

Snead, Bobbie. *Judge John B. Waldo: Oregon's John Muir*. Bend, OR: Maverick Publications, 2006.

Steen, Harold. *The U.S. Forest Service: A History*. Seattle: University of Washington Press, 1976.

Stuart, Allan, James Meacham, William Joy, Erik Steiner and Aileen Buckley. *Atlas of Oregon*. Corvallis: University of Oregon Press, 2002.

Sturtevant, William, and Deward Walker. *Handbook of North American Indians*. Vol 12. Washington, D.C.: Smithsonian Institution, 1998.

Sutter, Paul. *Driven Wild: How the Fight against Automobiles Launched the Modern Wilderness Movement*. Seattle: University of Washington Press, 2002.

Thomas, Jeff. *Oregon High: A Climbing Guide to Nine Cascade Volcanos*. Seattle: University of Washington Press, 1991.

Toedtemeier, Terry, and John Laursen. *Wild Beauty: Photographs of the Columbia River Gorge, 1867–1957*. Corvallis: Oregon State University Press, 2008.

White, Victor H. *The Story of Lige Coalman*. Sandy, OR: St. Paul's Press, 1972.

Williams, Gerald. "John B. Waldo and William Steel: Forest Reserve Advocates for the Cascade Range of Oregon." In *Origins of the National Forests: A Centennial Symposium*, edited by Harold K. Steen, 236–49. Durham, NC: Forest History Society, 1992.

———. *The U.S. Forest Service in the Pacific Northwest*. Corvallis: Oregon State University Press, 2009.

Winch, Martin. *Biography of a Place: Passages through a Central Oregon Meadow*. Bend, OR: Deschutes County Historical Society, 2006.

Woolley, Ivan. *Off to Mt. Hood: An Auto Biography of the Old Road*. Portland: Oregon Historical Society, 1959.

Young, Terence. *Heading Out: A History of American Camping*. Ithaca, NY: Cornell University Press, 2017.

## Newspapers and Periodicals

Barker, Stuart. "The Oregon Skyline Trail: Evolving Attitudes Toward Nature Tourism." *Oregon Historical Quarterly* 120, no. 1 (Spring 2019): 46–73.

*Bend (OR) Bulletin.* "Creation of a Great Public Park along Cascade Range Advised." February 22, 1922.

———. "Dee Wright." April 26, 1934.

———. "Feminine Trend on Skyline Trail Seen." August 31, 1922.

———. "New Bend Group Will Be Named Wednesday." December 20, 1927.

———. "On the Skyline." October 1, 1932.

———. "Two Men Start Ski Trip Down Oregon Skyline." February 18, 1948.

———. "Will Use Pictures as Road Propaganda." September 30, 1919.

*Bonneville (OR) Dam Chronicle.* "Skyline Trail Marked by New Signs." July 30, 1937.

*Capital Journal* (Salem, OR). "Judge Waldo Is Dead." September 3, 1907.

Cermak, Robert W. "Pioneering Aerial Forest Fire Control: The Army Air Patrol in California, 1919–1921." *California History* 70, no. 3 (Fall 1991): 290–305.

Clinton, Craig. "The Pictorial Maps of Fred A. Routledge." *Oregon Historical Quarterly* 117, no. 1 (Spring 2016): 38–75.

*Eastern Clackamas News* (Estacada OR). "The Skyline Trail." May 22, 1924.

Eaton, Walter Prichard. "On the Skyline Trail." *New York Times*, September 11, 1921.

*Eugene (OR) Guard.* "Beauty of Cascade Skyline Trail Shown in Film." December 7, 1941.

———. "Dee Wright Dies Here on Tuesday." April 24, 1934.

———. "Knowles Celebrate Golden Wedding." June 26, 1958.

———. "New Skyline Trail Being Built Nearer the Summit than Before." September 18, 1933.

———. "Skyline Trail Topic for Club Meeting Monday." March 23, 1936.

*Evening Herald* (Klamath Falls, OR). "Eight Groups to Trek on Famous Oregon Skyline." August 17, 1936.

———. "New Skyline Trail Map Is Distributed." December 8, 1931.

Fox, Stephen. "We Want No Straddlers." *Wilderness* 48, no. 167 (July 1984): 5–19.

Fuller, Virginia. "Couple Fulfill Dream and Take Off on Long Skyline Trail, Border to Border." *Herald & News* (Klamath Falls, OR), August 2, 1959.

Gildor, Dan. "Location, Location, Location: Forest Service Administration of the Recreation Residence Program." *Ecology Law Quarterly* 28, no. 4 (2002): 993–1,034.

Glover, James. "Romance, Recreation, and Wilderness: Influences on the Life and Work of Bob Marshall." *Environmental History Review* 14, no. 4 (Winter 1990): 22–39.

Hale, Jamie. "Now 100 Years Old, Eagle Creek Helped Revolutionize Camping in the 20th Century." *Oregonian* (Eugene, OR), July 14, 2016. www.oregonlive.com.

Hamlin, Annemarie. "The Greatest Ski Adventure." *1859 Magazine*, January 2010.

Harry, De Witt. "Close Rough View of Peak." *Sunday Oregonian* (Portland, OR), September 25, 1921.

*Herald and News* (Klamath Falls, OR). "Meissner Looks for Partner on Ski Trip." February 11, 1948.

Kelly, John W. "Oregon Roads Famous for Scenery." *Morning Oregonian* (Portland, OR), January 1, 1921.

Lalande, Jeff. "A Wilderness Journey with Judge John B. Waldo, Oregon's First Preservationist." *Oregon Historical Quarterly* 90, no. 2 (Summer 1989): 117–66.

Leopold, Aldo. "The Wilderness and Its Place in Forest Recreational Policy." *Journal of Forestry* 19, no. 7 (November 1921): 718–21.

MacKaye, Benton. "An Appalachian Trail: A Project in Regional Planning." *Journal of the American Institute of Architects* 9 (October 1921): 3–8.

Mann, Barney. "Across the Snowy Crest: Remembering the First Through-Ride of the Pacific Crest Trail, in 1959." *The Oregonian* (Portland, OR), September 25, 2009. www.oregonlive.com.

———. "Giving Trail History Its Due: The 1959 PCT Thru-Ride of Don and June Mulford." *PCT Communicator*, December 2009.

———. "Pacific Crest Trail Blazer Savors the Memories." *The Oregonian* (Portland, OR), July 24, 2011. www.oregonlive.com.

———. "Was This Swedish Immigrant the First Continental Divide Thru-Hiker?" *Backpacker Magazine*, January 2020.

Marshall, Robert. "The Problem of the Wilderness." *Scientific Monthly* 30, no. 2 (February 1930): 141–48.

Maxwell, Ben. "Waldo, Salem Jurist, Credited with Santiam Pass Discovery." *Capital Journal* (Salem, OR), March 23, 1948.

*Medford (OR) Mail Tribune*. "Girl Completes 2000-Mile Hike to Crater Lake." September 25, 1934.

Merriam, L.C. "The First Oregon Cavalry and the Oregon Central Military Road Survey of 1865." *Oregon Historical Quarterly* 60, no. 1 (March 1959): 89–124.

Minto, John. "Minto Pass: Its History, and Indian Tradition." *Quarterly of the Oregon Historical Society* 4, no. 3 (September 1903): 241–50.

———. "Youth to Age as an American." *Quarterly of the Oregon Historical Society* 9, no. 2 (June 1908): 127–72.

*Morning Oregonian* (Portland, OR). "Highway Plea Is Made." April 28, 1921.

———. "Proposed Skyline Road Through the Cascades' Grandeur Is Held Practical." January 1, 1920.

———. "Road Would Tap Scenic Wonderland." January 1, 1921.

———. "Skyline Trail Surveyed." September 5, 1934.

*Morning Register* (Eugene, OR). "Magazine Writer Will Take Hike over the Cascades." June 10, 1921.

Newman, Doug. "Book Examines Life of an Early Ranger." *Register-Guard* (Eugene, OR), June 5, 1988.

*Oregon Daily Journal* (Portland, OR). "Jefferson Park to Have Trails." September 11, 1919.

———. "Mazamas Return with Stories of Wonderful Hike." August 15, 1921.

———. "Oregon Country Realizes Dream of Camera Artist." October 12, 1919.

———. "Plans Progress to Complete Trails to Park at Crater Lake." October 12, 1919.

———. "The Skyline Trail." September 22, 1921.

*Oregon Statesman* (Salem, OR). "Anglers to Meet at Silverton." July 26, 1933.

*Oregon Sunday Journal* (Portland, OR). "Some Wonder Scenes Proposed Wonder Route Will Offer." January 16, 1921.

———. "$1,00,000 Will Build Highway Crater to Hood." November 7, 1921.

Rakestraw, Lawrence. "Sheep Grazing in the Cascade Range: John Minto vs. John Muir." *Pacific Historical Review* 27, no. 4 (November 1958): 371–82.

Roth, Dennis. "The National Forests and the Campaign for Wilderness Legislation." *Journal of Forest History* 28, no. 3 (July 1984): 112–25.

Sawyer, Robert. "Abbot Railroad Surveys, 1855." *Oregon Historical Quarterly* 33, no. 1 (March 1932): 1–24.

———. "Beginnings of McKenzie Highway, 1862." *Oregon Historical Quarterly* 31, no. 3 (September 1930): 261–68.

Steel, William Gladstone. "Judge Waldo Did It. Where Credit for Originating the Summit Reserve Belongs." *Oregonian* (Portland, OR), November 25, 1893.

Stivers, Vernon. "Saga of the Skyline Trail Recited." *The Sunday Oregonian* (Portland, OR), July 1, 1934.

*Sunday Oregonian* (Portland, OR). "Mazamas to Shift Summer Settings." June 19, 1921.

———. "Oregon Skyline Trail Rich in Rare Scenery." May 8, 1927.

———. "Park Promised by Forester Graves." July 18, 1915.

———. "Skyline Party Planned." June 23, 1929.

———. "Skyline Trail Would Open Scenic Wonders of the Cascades." January 6, 1921.

———. "Some Scenic Highways of the Future." April 13, 1924.

———. "Trip on the Skyline Evokes Interest." May 20, 1928.

Sutter, Paul. "A Blank Spot on the Map: Aldo Leopold, Wilderness, and U. S. Forest Service Recreational Policy, 1909–1924." *Western Historical Quarterly* 29, no. 2 (Summer 1998): 187–214.

Watters, Ron. "Jack Meissner and His Remarkable Ski Journey." *Cross Country Skier*, January 27, 2007.

Weiselberg, Erik. "He All but Made the Mountains: William Gladstone Steel, Mountain Climbing, and the Establishment of Crater Lake National Park." *Oregon Historical Quarterly* 103, no. 1 (Spring 2002): 50–75.

Wilkes, Charles. "Report on the Territory of Oregon." *Quarterly of the Oregon Historical Society* 12, no. 3 (September 1911): 269–99

## Documents, Reports, Maps and Legislation

Abbot, Henry. *Report of Lieut. Henry L. Abbot Upon Explorations for a Railroad Route from Sacramento Valley to the Columbia River*. Washington, D.C., 1857.

Abbot, Henry, and Robert Williamson. *Report of the Corps of Topographical Engineers upon Explorations for a Railroad Route from the Sacramento Valley to the Columbia River*. Washington D.C.: A.O.P. Nicholson, 1857.

Atwood, Kay, Sally Donovan, Dennis Gray and Ward Tonsfeldt. "Utility and Service Combined with Beauty: A Contextual and Architectural History of USDA Forest Service Region 6: 1905–1960." Bend, OR: U.S. Department of Agriculture, Forest Service Pacific Northwest Region, 2005.

Barker, Stuart J. "Through Oregon on High: The Construction and Consumption of Nature on the Oregon Skyline Trail." Master's thesis in American Studies, University of Kent, September 2014.

Beckham, Stephen. *Oregon Central Military Wagon Road: A History and Reconnaissance*. Eugene, OR; Willamette National Forest, 1981.

Cleator, Frederick. "History of the Oregon Skyline." 1941. Frederick William Cleator Papers. Box 1, Folder: "Organizations—Pacific Crest Trail Reports." Special Collections & University Archives, University of Oregon. Eugene, Oregon.

———. "Instructions for Extensive Examination and Report: Summer 1934." NARA, Seattle, Washington. Records of the U.S. Forest Service, Region 6.

———. Letter to A.D. Taylor. September 23, 1942. Frederick William Cleator Papers. Box 1, Folder: "Organizations—Pacific Crest Trail Reports." Special Collections & University Archives, University of Oregon. Eugene, Oregon.

———. Letter to Charles Paul Keyser, January 17, 1955. Frederick William Cleator Papers. Box 1, Folder: "Organizations—Pacific Crest Trail Reports." Special Collections & University Archives, University of Oregon. Eugene, Oregon.

———. Letter to Una Davies, Trails Club of Oregon, February 16, 1956. Frederick William Cleator Papers. Box 1, Folder: "Organizations—Pacific Crest Trail Reports." Special Collections & University Archives, University of Oregon. Eugene, Oregon.

———. "Recollections of Bob Marshall: Bob Marshall's Last Wilderness Adventure." Undated manuscript. Frederick William Cleator Papers. Box 1, Folder: "Organizations—Pacific Crest Trail Reports." Special Collections & University Archives, University of Oregon. Eugene, Oregon.

———. "Recreation Objectives." *Parks and Recreation* (May–June 1924): 467–75.

———. "Report of Preliminary Investigation Oregon Skyline Route." Willamette National Forest, Oregon, 1921.

———. "Skyline Diaries." Willamette National Forest, Oregon 1920.

———. "Status and Use of the Pacific Crest Trail," February 1941. Frederick William Cleator Papers. Box 1, Folder: "Organizations—Pacific Crest Trail

Reports." Special Collections & University Archives, University of Oregon. Eugene, Oregon.

———. "Summer Homes in the National Forests of Oregon and Washington." Seattle, WA: U.S. Forest Service, 1932.

———. "Tales of the Oregon Skyline: Diamond Lake Section." Undated manuscript. Frederick William Cleator Papers. Box 1, Folder: "Organizations—Pacific Crest Trail Reports." Special Collections & University Archives, University of Oregon. Eugene, Oregon.

Donovan, Sally, and Ward Tonsfeldt. "Mt. Hood National Forest Design Guidelines for Recreational Residences." Bend, OR: East Slope Cultural Services, January 2011.

Evans, Gail. "Historic Resource Study: Olympic National Park Washington." Seattle, WA: Department of the Interior, National Park Service, 1983.

Gray, Gary. "Radio for the Fireline: A History of Electronic Communication in the Forest Service, 1905–1975." Washington, D.C.: United States Department of Agriculture, Forest Service, March 1982.

Henthorne, Mary C. "The Three Sisters Outing, 1916." *Mazama Annual* 5, no. 1 (December 1916): 7–23.

Holstine, Craig and Robin Bruce. "An Historical Overview of the Wenatchee National Forest." Cheney, WA: U.S. Department of Agriculture, Forest Service, Pacific Northwest Region. and Historical Services, 1994.

Houser, Michael. "A Prehistoric Overview of Deschutes County." Salem, OR: Oregon State Historic Preservation Office, 1996.

Hoyt, Hugh Myron. "The Good Roads Movement in Oregon: 1900–1920." PhD. dissertation, University of Oregon, Eugene, OR, 1966.

Krechel, Frances, ed. "The Forest Service and Cy J. Bingham." Vol 1. Hemet, CA. Unpublished manuscript, 1984.

Marshall, Robert. "The Forest for Recreation." *A Plan for American Forestry. Letter from the Secretary of Agriculture Transmitting in Response to S. Res. 175 (72nd Congress) the Report of the Forest Service of the Agricultural Department on the Forest Problem of the United States.* Washington, D.C.: U.S. Government Printing Office, 1933.

———. Letter to Frederick Cleator, October 2, 1939. Frederick William Cleator Papers (Identifier: Ax 013) Box 1, Folder: "Organizations—Pacific Crest Trail Reports." Special Collections & University Archives, University of Oregon. Eugene, Oregon.

McClelland, Linda. "Presenting Nature: The Historic Landscape Design of the National Park Service, 1916 to 1942." Washington D.C.: National Park Service, 1993.

Minor, Rick, and Audrey Frances Pecor. *Cultural Resource Overview of the Willamette National Forest Western Oregon.* Eugene: University of Oregon, 1977.

Mitchell, Ryan Franklin. "Ambivalent Landscapes: An Historical Geography of Recreation and Tourism on Mount Hood, Oregon." Paper 2227 (2005). Dissertations and Theses. Portland State University. Department of Geography. Portland, OR.

Oregon Department of Fish and Wildlife. *Oregon Conservation Strategy*. Salem, OR, 2016.

Oregon Department of Transportation. "History of State Highways in Oregon." Salem, OR, March 2020.

Oregon Tourist and Information Bureau. "Oregon Skyline Trail Map: Mt. Hood to Crater Lake." Portland, OR (1921).

Oregon Trails Coordinating Council. *Oregon Historic Trails Report*. Salem, OR, May 1998.

Otis, Alison, William Honey, Thomas Hogg and Kimberly Lakin. "The Forest Service and The Civilian Conservation Corps: 1933–42." Washington, D.C.: United States Department of Agriculture, August 1986.

Outdoor Recreation Resources Review Commission, Laurance S. Rockefeller, Chairman. *Outdoor Recreation for America: A Report to the President and to the Congress*, January 1962.

Parker, Alfred F. "The Twenty-Ninth Annual Mazama Outing: The Three Sisters." *Mazama Annual* 6, no. 3 (December 1922): 7–20.

Rakestraw, Lawrence. "A History of Forest Conservation in the Pacific Northwest, 1891–1913." PhD diss., Department of History, University of Washington. Reprinted by Arno Press, New York, 1979.

Rakestraw, Lawrence, and Mary Rakestraw. *History of the Willamette National Forest*. U.S. Department of Agriculture, U.S. Forest Service, Willamette National Forest, Eugene, Oregon, 1991.

*Reports of Explorations and Surveys, to Ascertain the Most Practicable and Economical Route for a Railroad from the Mississippi River to the Pacific Ocean*. Washington, D.C.: Thomas H. Ford, 1860

Riddell, H.H. "Three Sisters Outing." *Mazama Annual* 4, no. 1 (1912): 10–20.

Rogue River–Siskiyou National Forest. "Rogue River—Siskiyou National Forest Roads Analysis." Medford, OR: U.S. Forest Service, January 2004.

Royer, William. "Skyline Trail: 1934 Reconnaissance." U.S. Forest Service, Region 6. November 15, 1934.

Stark, Peter. "The Mapping of Our National Forests." Milford, PA: Grey Towers Heritage Association, 2020.

———. "Names, Boundaries, and Maps: A Resource for the Historical Geography of the National Forest System of the United States, The Pacific Northwest Region." Milford, PA: Grey Towers Heritage Association, 2020.

Thompson, Gail, Steve Wilke and Glen Lindeman. *Cultural Resource Overview for Land and Resource Management Planning on the Winema National Forest*. Seattle, WA: Geotechnical Consultants, 1979.

Throop, Gail. "Recreation Development in the National Forests in Oregon and Washington 1905–1945." USDA Forest Service, Pacific Northwest Regional Office, Portland, Oregon, 2004.

Tweed, William. *A History of Outdoor Recreation Development in National Forests: 1891–1942*. Clemson: SC: Clemson University, 1989.

———. "Recreation Site Planning and Improvements in National Forests: 1891–1942." Washington, D.C.: U.S. Department of Agriculture, 1980.

Unrau, Harlan D. *Administrative History of Crater Lake National Park*. Vols. 1 and 2. Washington, DC: National Park Service, 1986.

U.S. Congress. National Trails System Act, October 2, 1968; PL. 90-543, 82 Stat. 919, 16 U.S.C. §§ 124l-51.

U.S. Department of the Interior. *Trails for America: Report on the Nationwide Trail Study*. Washington, D.C., 1965.

U.S. Forest Service. "Diamond Lake Recreational Residence Tract Umpqua National Forest." Portland, OR: Region 6, Pacific Northwest Regional Office, January 2021.

Vora, Rachel. "The History of the Recreation Residence Program on the Deschutes National Forest." Undergraduate thesis, University of Oregon–Bend, 2009.

Waldo, John Breckenridge. Journals and Letters, August 7, 1884. Title: John Breckenridge Waldo Papers. Identifier: Col 303. Box 2: Typescript copies of journals and letters, 1880–1907. Special Collections & University Archives, University of Oregon. Eugene, Oregon.

Waugh, Frank. "Landscape Engineering in the National Forests." Washington, D.C.: Government Printing Office, 1918.

———. "Recreational Uses on the National Forests." Washington, D.C.: Government Printing Office, 1917.

Williams, Gerald. "The Civilian Conservation Corps, 1933–1942." January 14, 2003. *Gerald W. Williams Papers*. Series 1: Williams Manuscripts, 1985–2005. Digital File 1.11. Special Collections and Archives Research Center, Oregon State University. Corvallis, Oregon.

———. "Expeditions, Explorations, and Journeys into and through the Regions of Western Oregon, 1805–1869." May 27, 2000. *Gerald W. Williams Papers*. Series 1: Williams Manuscripts, 1985–2005. Digital File 1.32. Special Collections and Archives Research Center, Oregon State University. Corvallis, Oregon.

———, ed. *Judge John Breckenridge Waldo: Letters and Journals from the High Cascades of Oregon, 1880–1907*. Roseburg: Umpqua National Forest, 1986.

Williams, Gerald, and Stephen Mark. *Establishing and Defending the Cascade Range Forest Reserve: As Found in the Letters of William G. Steel, John B. Waldo and Others Supplemented by Newspapers, Magazines, and Official Reports, 1885–1912.* Portland, OR: U.S. Forest Service, 1995.

## *Digital Resources and Websites*

Bassett, Karen, Jim Renner and Joyce White. "Klamath Trail." Oregon Trails Coordinating Council, 1998. https://historicoregoncity.org.

Brock, Mathew, and Jack Grauer. "Mazamas." *Oregon Encyclopedia*, June 9, 2022. www.oregonencyclopedia.org.

Building Oregon. "Cabin, Camp Sherman Recreational Residences (Camp Sherman, Oregon)." University of Oregon. *Oregon Digital*. https://oregondigital.org.

Cain, Allen. "LaGrande-Wallowa Lake Highway, 1923." *Oregon History Project*. www.oregonhistoryproject.org.

Caldbick, John. "Frederick William Cleator (1883–1957)." *History Link*. January 30, 2012. www.historylink.org.

Clark, William et al. *The Journals of the Lewis and Clark Expedition*. Edited by Gary Moulton. Lincoln, NE: University of Nebraska Press / University of Nebraska-Lincoln Libraries-Electronic Text Center, 2005. http://lewisandclarkjournals.unl.edu.

Colburn, Don. "Mary Carolyn Davies." *Oregon Encyclopedia*. September 13, 2022. www.oregonencyclopedia.org.

Deacon, Kristine. "Birds Come to the Rescue of Rangers Battling Oregon Wildfires." *Oregon State Archives*. October 13, 2020. www.facebook.com.

Frémont, John Charles, John James Abert and Millard Fillmore. *Map of an Exploring Expedition to the Rocky Mountains in the Year and to Oregon & North California in the Years 1843–44.* Washington, D.C., 1844.

Howell, Kenny. "Exploring the History of the Pacific Crest Trail." *The Trek*, February 18, 2019. https://thetrek.com.

Joslin, Les. "Cyrus Bingham." *Oregon Encyclopedia*, February 3, 2021. www.oregonencyclopedia.org.

"Kiser Photo Company." *Archives West*. Accessed June 8, 2023. https://archiveswest.orbiscascade.org.

Lalande, Jeff. "Aerial Forest-Fire Patrol Program in Oregon, 1919–1927." *Oregon Encyclopedia* March 11, 2022. www.oregonencyclopedia.org.

———. "John B. Waldo." *Oregon Encyclopedia*, November 22, 2022. www.oregonencyclopedia.org.

Lewis, David. "Ethnographic Molalla Homelands in Historic Scholarship." *Quartux Journal*, October 21, 2018. https://ndnhistoryresearch.com.

———. "Outside the Ethnographic Box: Native Trade Networks." *Quartux Journal*, June 3, 2016. https://ndnhistoryresearch.com.

Lindberg, Kathy. "Santiam Pass Ski Lodge." U.S. Forest Service. www.fs.usda.gov.

Mann, Barney. "The Making of the First Pacific Crest Trail Guidebook." *PCT Communicator*, February 2010. www.pcta.org.

———. "No, It's Montgomery." *PCT Communicator*, March 2011. www.pcta.org.

Mansayon, Christopher. "Henry Yelkus." *Oregon Encyclopedia*, November 3, 2022. www.oregonencyclopedia.org.

Mark, Stephen. "Frederick William Cleator (1883–1957)." *Oregon Encyclopedia*, September 21, 2022. www.oregonencyclopedia.org.

———. "On an Old Road to Crater Lake." *Crater Lake National Park Nature Notes* 28 (1997). http://npshistory.com.

———. "William Gladstone Steel." *Oregon Encyclopedia*, November 22, 2022. www. oregonencyclopedia.org.

Nye, Nancy C. "Camping in the National Forests." *Forest Society*. Accessed May 30, 2023. https://foresthistory.org.

Oregon Department of Transportation. "The Historic Columbia River Highway." 2013. www.oregon.gov.

Oregon State Highway Commission. "Tentative Plan for the State Highway System of Oregon, 1916." Oregon Maps Digital Collection. https://scarc.library. oregonstate.edu.

Pacific Crest Trail Association. "Founders of the Pacific Crest Trail." Accessed July 10, 2023. www.pcta.org.

Pater, David, et al. *Ecoregions of Western Washington and Oregon*. Reston, VA: U.S. Geological Survey, 1998.

President Lyndon Johnson, February 8, 1965, "Special Message to Congress on Conservation and Restoration of Natural Beauty." American Presidency Project. www.presidency.ucsb.edu.

Sherrod, David. "Cascade Mountain Range in Oregon." *Oregon Encyclopedia*, November 10, 2021. www.oregonencyclopedia.org.

Walker, James. "Cartography of Oregon." *Oregon Encyclopedia*, November 9, 2022. www.oregonencyclopedia.org.

Williams, Gerald. "McKenzie Pass." *Oregon Encyclopedia*, June 13, 2022. www. oregonencyclopedia.org.

———. "The USDA Forest Service—The First Century." Washington, D.C.: USDA Forest Service, 2000. http://npshistory.com.

———. "Willamette Pass." *Oregon Encyclopedia*, September 30, 2022. www. oregonencyclopedia.org.

Young, Robert. "Mount Hood from Tysch Prairie." *Oregon Historical Society*. www. oregonhistoryproject.org.

Zenk, Henry. "Molalla Peoples." *Oregon Encyclopedia*, August 15, 2022. www. oregonencyclopedia.org.

# INDEX

# ABOUT THE AUTHOR

**G**lenn Voelz served for twenty-five years in the U.S. Army as an intelligence officer and spent over a decade living and working across Asia, Europe, the Middle East and Africa. He held senior leadership positions at the Pentagon, in the White House Situation Room and at NATO headquarters in Brussels, Belgium. Glenn is a graduate of the United States Military Academy at West Point and served on the faculty as an assistant professor in the Department of History. He is the author of two previous books on Oregon history.